MEANINGFUL FLESH

Fig. 1. Hieronymus Bosch, *Ship of Fools* (1490–1500)

First published in 2018 by punctum books, Earth, Milky Way.
https://punctumbooks.com

ISBN-13: 978-1-947447-32-5 (print)
ISBN-13: 978-1-947447-33-2 (ePDF)

LCCN: 2017957481
Library of Congress Cataloging Data is available from the Library of Congress

Copy editing: Andy Doty
Interior design: Vincent W.J. van Gerven Oei
Cover design: Chris Piuma
Cover image: Ernst Haeckel, *Kunstformen der Natur* (1904),
    plate 8: Discomedusae

HIC SVNT MONSTRA

Meaningful Flesh

Reflections on Religion and Nature for a
Queer Planet

Whitney A. Bauman, editor

Contents

Queering Religion and Nature

Religion is much queerer than we ever imagined. Nature is as well. These are the two basic insights that have led to this book: we hope to queerly go where no thinkers have gone before. The combination of queer theory and religion has been happening for at least 25 years. People such as John Boswell began to examine the history of religious traditions with a queer eye, and soon after we had the indecent theology of Marcella Althaus Ried. Jay Johnston, one of the authors in this volume, is among those who have used the queer eye to interrogate authority within Christian theological traditions. At the same time, interrogating nature from a queer perspective has begun, perhaps most notably in the work of Joan Roughgarden's *Evolution's Rainbow* and with the works of Anne Fausto-Sterling. However, the intersections of religion, nature, and queer theory have largely been left untouched. With the exception of Dan Spencer, the author of the Introduction for this volume and one of the early pioneers in this realm of thought with his book *Gay and Gaia,* and Greta Gaard, whose work is developing a queer ecofeminist thought, authors have largely ignored religion and nature or religion and ecology in the realm of queer theory.

In part, the blinders to queer theory on the part of eco-thinkers (religious or otherwise) are the same as the blinders eco-thinkers have when it comes to postmodern thought in general:

namely, if there are no foundations, how does one create an environmental ethic or a "nature" to save? Do we really have time to be dealing with all of these theoretical issues when the earth is in the midst of the sixth mass extinction and a rapidly changing climate? Obviously, the authors in this volume think it is important and that these questions need new responses and thoughts unprecedented in comparison to previous ones. In broad strokes, the authors agree that queer theory has something to tell us about how to live to achieve a better planetary future.

For this reason and many others, the current volume on religion, nature, and queer theory is quite groundbreaking. Carol Wayne White starts us off with the issue of race, religion, and queer theory and how together they might help to develop an African-American Religious Naturalism. Jake Erickson's piece provides us with a fascinating combination of Isabella Rossellini's "Green Porno" and Martin Luther's thought in order to develop an indecent theology. Continuing on the theological theme, Jay Johnston's "Master and Pup" helps to open up the *imago Dei* (or what it means to be "made in the image of God") to the more-than-human world and to rethink theologically the status of non-human animals. My own chapter attempts to look at climate change, globalization, and queer theory as the grounds for new possibilities for planetary becoming. And finally, eco-critic Timothy Morton, whose seminal essay "Queer Ecology" is so important for these intersections of thought, develops a critique of "agrologistics" in dialogue with queer theory and postmodern thought.

Though these essays span many different disciplines and themes, they are all held together by the triple focus on religion, nature, and queer theory. Some focus more on one of those loci than the others, but all of them at least mix with each of them. They can be read in order, out of order, together, or as individual reflections. There is no right or wrong way to engage with the chapters in this book, but hopefully engaging with them in some way will help inspire new ways of thinking about (and perhaps even becoming in) the world for you, just as they have for me. Without being too ambitious, I hope that these essays help to open up a whole new trajectory of conversation at the intersection of religion, nature, and queer theory.

As with all books, this one too only appears as a result of a lot of work both seen and unseen. In addition to the countless activists and academicians who have come before us, paving the way for such a volume, I'd like to thank a few groups of people more specifically. First and foremost, I'd like to thank the authors of this volume for seeing the project through to publication. Secondly, I'd like to thank my colleagues and friends at Florida International University, at the Religion and Ecology Group of the American Academy of Religion, at the Forum on Religion and Ecology, and at the International Society for the Study of Religion, Nature and Culture. Without the fruitful conversations that have happened in these spaces this volume would not have emerged. Third, I want to thank the anonymous reviewers of earlier versions of these chapters; without their critical insights these essays would not be as complete as they are. Fourth and finally, I'd like to thank the editorial team at punctum books for taking an interest in this volume and seeing it through to publication.

— Whitney A. Bauman

Religion, Nature, and Queer Theory

Daniel T. Spencer

In 1989 I began doctoral work at Union Theological Seminary to integrate insights from ecology, liberation theologies, and ecofeminism — what eventually emerged was my book, *Gay and Gaia: Ethics, Ecology and the Erotic.* I now welcome this opportunity to look back at how the emerging intersections among religion, nature, culture, and sexuality in the 1980s and 1990s shaped those reflections, and to look forward to the insights of a new generation of queer scholars of religion.

Trained as a geologist who came late to theology and ethics, my intuitions about this intersection began to form in college when I studied volcanoes in Costa Rica in 1978 as a deeply closeted gay man. Here I was exposed to human rights issues and poverty, exacerbated by the many civil wars engulfing Costa Rica's neighbors. I first enrolled at Union in 1980 to try to address the many theoethical issues that my time in Central America and my closeted sexuality were raising, having little inclination then how deeply intertwined the answers would become. Having recently come out to family and friends, I returned to Costa Rica in 1982 to study liberation theology. I spent my weekends working with refugee children from El Salvador, displaced from their homelands by the combination of military violence and ecological degradation from the scorched earth tactics of US-sponsored counterinsurgency tactics. Coming to terms with my own gay identity has therefore always been deeply intertwined with my love of the earth and its diverse ecosystems and my commitment to social justice for the poor and exploited.

Gay and Gaia was my effort to integrate the insights of ecology and environmental ethics with liberation theologies — particularly gay and lesbian, black, Latin American, and feminist — and ecofeminism. I was largely unexposed to the emerging field of queer theory at this time; Robert Goss's important book, *Jesus Acted Up: A Gay and Lesbian Manifesto,* came out in 1993 and began the important work of integrating queer insights with theology but did not address ecology and environmental concerns so central to my own commitments. I was more influenced by the pioneering work in gay theology of my friend J. Michael Clark, whose prophetic *A Place to Start: Toward an Unapologetic Gay Liberation Theology* appeared in 1989 just as I began my doctoral studies. By 1993 Clark had published *Beyond Our Ghettos: Gay Theology in Ecological Perspective,* the first work I know of to try to articulate a "gay ecotheological paradigm." Deeply influenced by the ecosocial crisis of HIV/AIDS, Clark's work remains for me some of the most prophetic and profound reflections on the intersections of religion, nature and queer theory.

In *Gay and Gaia* I tried to address several issues. Convinced of a profound "sense of the sacred found in the interconnectedness of all," I sought to shift the grounding for ethics from "an anthropocentric, human-centered worldview" to an "ecocentric, all-of-life centered worldview." Methodologically I was convinced that ecology, liberation theologies, and ecofeminism all had critical insights to building an ethic of sustainability that could integrate all levels of our lives, from our most intimate relationships ("Gay") to the planetary ("Gaia"). Key to this was reclaiming *eros* as the life-force of attraction that informs all our relations, and I argued that gay and lesbian experience and theory make critical contributions for how to do this. As a way to locate this work conceptually, I coined the concept of "ecological location," enlarging the concept of social location to include both where human beings are located within human society and within the broader biotic community, as well as conceiving other members of the biotic community and the biotic community itself as locatable active agents that historically interact with and shape the other members of the ecological community, including human beings (Spencer 1996: 295–96).

Without the explicit theoretical tools that would emerge in queer theory, I intuited that key to this project would be deconstructing rigid dualistic and binary constructs that informed theological notions of God, nature, and humanity, and the relationship (or lack thereof) among them.

Since writing *Gay and Gaia,* two other sets of experiences have strongly shaped my thinking on these issues. In 1993 I started teaching as an openly gay religion professor at Drake University, helping undergraduates negotiate the perils of coming out while they explored queering their identities. Struck by the overwhelming whiteness of Iowa in contrast to its Native American histories and origins, I examined the reality and construct of race through the lenses of ecological location and the settlement history of Iowa to conceptualize race as an *ecological* construct. It embeds within it a racialized history of interacting with the natural world that reflects the dynamics of historical racism and exploitation.[1] It is thus a particular delight to read Carol Wayne White's essay here on James Baldwin and constructing a queer African-American religious naturalism.

In 2000, I moved to Montana and later joined the Environmental Studies program at the University of Montana where I shifted my teaching and research to ethical issues of globalization and ecological restoration while retaining a liberationist commitment. This shift in my own ecological location has sensi-

---

1   This in turn informs part of my current work of reconceiving the practice of ecological restoration as one of ecological *reparations* to address the paired exploitation and injustices of the degradation and loss of native ecosystems and peoples.

tized me to important connections in queer theory and emerging trends in postmodern thought — particularly destabilizing and deconstructing fixed categories undergirding modernity with ecological perspectives. The impact of chaos theory on ecology, the emergence of hybrid and novel ecosystems that increasingly make up our postmodern ecological locations, the destabilizing impacts of climate change, and the shift in ecological restoration from trying to restore to the past to restoring damaged ecosystems to multiple possible future trajectories — all suggest promising and important intersections between religion, nature, and queer theory. Within this framework, I am currently exploring a shift from a more static ethics of sustainability that informed *Gay and Gaia* to a more dynamic *restorative* paradigm that honors human and more-than-human agencies and its ecosocial implications for living well in the Anthropocene.

The essays in this book push our reflections and praxis at the intersection of religion, nature, and queer theory in important and exciting ways. The genius of these chapters is that once read, we can never look at or think about the subjects of each in quite the same way — queer(y)ing opens up new and transformative possibilities, so critical in the perilous times of the Anthropocene. While each essay makes its own distinctive contribution, the queer notion of "performativity" links them in several ways.

Carol Wayne White examines ecosystems of queer affection in the writings of James Baldwin to ground an emerging African-American religious naturalism. Baldwin coined metaphors of "bastard" and "freak" to "illuminate the complicated intersections of queerness, blackness, and religious rhetoric" in order to expose and undermine white supremacy that "established white male heterosexuality as the norm for ascertaining and evaluating other expressions of desire." Against the fixed binaries that both white supremacy and traditional Black church religiosity use to police queer desire, White draws "the contours of a queer African-American religious topography where polyamorous bastards roam ecstatically in nomadic desiring." This "pleasurable 'roaming' of a queer love" in turn "celebrates humans' radical relationality with each other, and, with other natural processes," revealing our common humanity as an ongoing task that we construct rather than a fixed essence we discover.

Jacob Erickson takes "a constructive posture of irreverence" to destabilize the concepts of "God" and "Nature" in contemporary ecotheology. Queering Martin Luther's view of incarnation, Erickson "offers the potential for a queer incarnation of divinity in which that divinity is caught up — and even plays several roles — in the performative indeterminacy of the earth and of the cosmos." From this irreverent and playful queerying of sacred notions, "divinity becomes a 'queer critter' seducing other queer critters' disturbing loves and ever-new responsibilities." All theology is thus both irreverent and queer: "Our language, speaking of God and creation, is carnivalesque, topsy-turvy, performative, animated, vibrant, constantly changing shape and drag."

Jay Johnson's reflection emerges from a multi-year relationship with his dog, Tyler, who helps him to realize that queer theorizing can move beyond critical interrogation of gender and sexuality "to humanity's deeply contested relationship with other animals." Blurring lines between human and dog, master and pet, he examines the multiple performativities in ecosystems of gay affection and particularly the human-pup-play phenomenon in some sectors of gay life. In a recent 'pupumentary,' Master Skip and Pup Tim perform other-than-human behaviors and roles to blur the human-animal binary and open up possibilities of "cultivating inter-species relationships of empathy and intimacy." Johnson reflects on their experience to deconstruct rigid anthropocentric doctrines of the *imago Dei* that allow Christians to ignore critical issues of "evolutionary theodicy" and the pervasiveness of suffering throughout the animal world.

Whitney Bauman draws on queer theory to engage new possibilities of performance that decenter anthropocentrism and open up ways to re-engage with/on/in the planet by respecting its agency at multiple levels. Connecting with my own work on the twin "wicked problems" of globalization and climate change, Bauman skillfully "queers the planet" to enable us to "break out of the thought habits of modern scientific reduction" and "the habits of becoming according to the laws of capitalist reproduction." Becoming versatile in planetary ethics requires reflexive positioning to discern "the contexts and contours of our planetary becoming."

Timothy Morton begins his essay by queering the "law of noncontradiction" that permeates western thought dating at least to Aristotle through the notion of performativity where phenomena simultaneously and paradoxically are and are not what they seem. He undermines the rigid "agrilogistics" and the persistent acts of violence needed to maintain it that emerged in the Neolithic and continue to structure society in the modern era. In contrast, queer green thinking and acting subverts agrilogistics, as do "the uncontainable enjoyment" of queer sex and the playfulness of toys, opening up vital new possibilities for our time. Hence, "thinking ecologically precisely means thinking that things are queer green toys" that can move us past the violent binaries continuously policed and enforced to maintain the [now globalized] structures of agrilogistics.

I hope these diverse essays queer your imagination and open up new possibilities for queer praxes of liberation as they have my own.

References

Clark, J. Michael. 1993. *Beyond Our Ghettos: Gay Theology in Ecological Perspective*. Cleveland: Pilgrim Press.

———. 1989. *A Place to Start: Toward an Unapologetic Gay Liberation Theology*. Dallas: Monument Press.

Goss, Robert. 1993. *Jesus Acted Up: A Gay and Lesbian Manifesto*. San Francisco: HarperSanFrancisco.

Spencer, Daniel T. 1996. *Gay and Gaia: Ethics, Ecology and the Erotic*. Cleveland: Pilgrim Press.

CHAPTER 1

Polyamorous Bastards: James Baldwin's Opening to a Queer African-American Religious Naturalism

Carol Wayne White

> *Love takes off masks that we fear we cannot live*
> *without and know we cannot live within.*
> — James Baldwin

At the height of the civil rights era in the twentieth century, James Baldwin poignantly described blacks' experiences of marginality in North America. In a country besieged by white supremacy, he tried to capture the acute sense of displacement felt by African Americans with the creative use of the "bastard" epithet. In doing so, he drew richly from formative familial experiences and the black holiness tradition of his youth. Having never known his biological father and feeling estranged from his emotionally distant stepfather — a factory worker and storefront preacher whom his mother married when he was three — Baldwin would later write about the anguish of experiencing life as an "illegitimate" kid. In both acclaimed novels and critical essays, he creatively used the bastard motif to augment a critical self-awareness associated with being the outsider and the illegitimate other.

Conjoining the personal and the political, Baldwin rhetorically expanded the term bastard to convey blacks' harried existence in the "New World" and to evoke an ethical quandary for white Americans. In the absence of embodied authenticity and relational integrity, Baldwin's bastard metaphor revealed the pathology inherent in many whites' refusal to embrace their familial kinship with blacks. With this term, Baldwin also raised a critical question to the America of his day: whether hope for its future could possibly exist in light of distorted forms of relationality. Baldwin's very use of the bastard term symbolized the moral paralysis he saw embedded in an American psyche suffering from a great lie perpetuated by white supremacy.

Baldwin's use of the bastard metaphor has elicited a range of critical responses, from Cornel West's distrust of a perceived apolitical individualism to Clarence Hardy's declaration that Baldwin was poignantly seeking recognition from whites (West 1982; Hardy 2003, 105). However, I consider Baldwin's use of it as part of a complex ontological project with monumental social, affective, and ethical implications. With the bastard motif, Baldwin also underscored impoverished views of humanity kept in place by polarized, binary constructions (e.g., white/black, insider/outsider, superiority/inferiority, the saved/damned, hetero-normative/homo-depraved beings).

In an attempt to address these various forms of alienation experienced by Americans desiring profound connection with otherness, Baldwin introduced the concept of love. Far from being a lofty abstraction, Baldwin's conception of love entailed a radical re-adjustment of human relations, requiring individuals and communities to embrace others they often feared, dismissed, or even hated. This specific form of love demanded from whites and blacks unprecedented acts of courage and audacious choices. Accordingly, his view of love was a creative means of synthesizing the affective and ethical with socio-political advancements.

In this chapter, I explore the rich conceptual space opened by Baldwin's use of the bastard metaphor and his ensuing concept of love. In describing Baldwin's usage of this term, I focus primarily on cultural critiques found in his critical essays; I also use Baldwin's writings as an opening for articulating my fuller explication of queer religious naturalism. Inspired by his creative reach, I thus specify bastard as a trope to mark the emergence of an African-American religious naturalism that resists normative (and, in my rendering, impoverished) views of our humanity. Specifically, in negating pauperized views of blacks' humanity perpetuated by white supremacy, this African-American religious naturalism invites contemporary readers to reconsider who and what we are: value-laden natural processes that become human in specific orientations. It presupposes human animals' deep, inextricable homology with each other, drawing our attention to an expansive view of our humanity as an emergent phenomenon, not an achievement. Further, in underscoring humans' inexhaustible connection or entanglement with other natural processes, this naturalistic view also brings to light our essential connection with the more-than-human that constitutes the very notion of the human as such.[1]

Further, building on a notion of love that I glean from Baldwin's self-understanding as an (sexualized) outsider, my view of religiosity celebrates nomadic, polyamorous relations. With its naturalistic grounding, this model of religiosity resists the "isms" based on binary constructions that uphold asymmetrical relationships and polarize our desire for connection with all

---

1   Utilizing the tenets of religious naturalism in conjunction with values discourse, I consider humans' awareness and appreciation of our connection to "all that is" as an expression of what we perceive as ultimately important and valuable. Since religious naturalism does not use "supernatural" concepts or theories in comprehending humans' need for value and meaning, the realm of nature is the focus (this includes both natural processes and human culture for most religious naturalists). Religious naturalists draw on two fundamental convictions in understanding basic human quests for meaning and value: the sense of Nature's richness, spectacular complexity, and fertility, and the recognition that Nature is the only realm in which people live out their lives.

that is. In so doing, this African-American religious naturalism adopts a queer positionality — or what Michael Warner has described as resistance "to regimes of the normal" (Warner 1993, xxvii). As queer enactment, this African-American religiosity calls for a radical relationality in which our experiences of love overcome arbitrary boundaries held in place by normalizing cultural markers. It seeks a modality of existence based in transformation; in such a vision, our expanded humanity as sentient beings is porous — we suffuse each other with care and a sense of belonging together.

To advance my argument, I first introduce Baldwin's cultural critiques that gave rise to the bastard motif and discuss his creative use of the term in specific contexts. These brief discussions serve as an opening to my fuller explorations of the term in a queer religious context. I then highlight Baldwin's rejection of a model of Christianity that gloried a depraved blackness with its theistic symbolism of a white God. Of key importance here are Baldwin's warnings against investing in a religious vision that implicitly kept in place white racist constructs, problematic cultural practices, and heteronormative values. Following this, I discuss Baldwin's concept of embodied love, which he viewed as a corrective to the normative religious system. Finally, I explore the possibility of a queer African-American religious naturalism that advances Baldwin's notion of enacting boundless love with each other. Given the historical gap between Baldwin's and our own time, I attempt to sketch a capacious model of African-American religiosity that he was unable to conceive at that time. In order to distinguish this religious perspective as queer enactment, I incorporate insights from Claudia Schippert's strategy of queering the religious discipline. My goal is to draw the contours of a queer African-American religious topography where polyamorous bastards roam ecstatically in nomadic desiring.

Baldwin's Bastards: Illicit Race and Nomadic Sensibilities

Baldwin emerged as an essayist in the fifties when the civil-rights movement was barely in discernible form. In his first collection of essays, *Notes of a Native Son* (1955), followed by *Nobody Knows My Name* (1961) and *The Fire Next Time* (1963), Baldwin introduced a style of writing that fused in a unique fashion the personal, the political, and the literary. Whether recounting his experiences as a teenage preacher, a queer male, a black expatriate, a public intellectual, or an activist in the struggle for civil rights, Baldwin wrote passionately about the quandaries of living life as an outlier.[2] He brought an intense self-awareness to his inhabiting within one body many different (and often excluded) cultural markers.

In the America of his day, these identities were persistently viewed as oppositional: his blackness and erotic-affective desires; his precocious religious insights and radical activism; his designation as a black American artist in Europe juxtaposed with his European celebrity in white America. In his quest to create an authentic mode of existence, however, Baldwin resisted, with varying degrees of success, the easy option of reducing his capacious humanity to any single identity. Furthermore, he creatively expanded this sensibility to include the collective experiences of African Americans as he sought new ways of being in which he and others could live fully with perceived differences (White 2016, 95).

In their introduction to a critical collection of essays on Baldwin, Cora Kaplan and Bill Schwartz described a dominant trend in Baldwin studies that often failed to understand this point. As they observed: "For too long one Baldwin has been pitted against another Baldwin, producing a series of polarities that has skewed our understanding: his art against his politics, his fiction against his nonfiction; his early writings against his late writings; American Baldwin against European Baldwin; black Baldwin against queer Baldwin" (Kaplan and Schwartz 2011, 3). I share this robust reading of Baldwin. Select essays show Baldwin resisting facile, externally imposed views of his humanity, as

---

2 Parts of this discussion are adapted from my chapter on James Baldwin in *Black Lives and Sacred Humanity* (New York: Fordham University Press, 2016).

well as that of other blacks. He opened an imaginative space in which North Americans entrapped in isolationist encampments could be free and re-envision themselves as relational beings capable of living with difference. In the 1984 introduction to *Notes of a Native Son,* Baldwin described the menacing effects of racialized living in America. Symbolically, socially, and materially, human lives were affected by a problematic cultural system that elevated certain bodies over others, ultimately leaving all alienated from each other.

For Baldwin, racialized existence in its most extreme form was expressed in a black-white oppositional logic that was omnipresent: "The conundrum of color is the inheritance of every American, be he/she legally or actually Black or White. It is a fearful inheritance, for which untold multitudes, long ago, sold their birthright. Multitudes are doing so, until today" (Baldwin 1998, 810).[3] His writings reverberate with the conundrum of affirming life and embracing one's humanity in a world (or culture of values) that one has not created. As such, they reveal an important observation about black lives in America that Frederick Douglass articulated in the nineteenth century when addressing the National Colored Convention of 1853: "Our white fellow-country men do not know us. They are strangers to our character, ignorant of our capacity, oblivious of our history and progress, and are misinformed as to the principles and ideas that control and guide us as a people. The great mass of American citizens estimate us as being a characterless and purposeless people" (Douglass 2000, 269).

---

3   Given the historical framework in which Baldwin was writing, his critiques target a problematic, limited binary constituted by the symbolic notions of whiteness and blackness. As current Critical Race Theory suggests, however, racist discourse emerges from the dominance of a white supremacist ideology, or a master narrative that has failed to include the value and experiences of all groups whose identities have been isolated from and seen as distinct from "white" skin and everything associated with this distinction. In my broader work on religious naturalism, I emphasize this broader notion of racialized discourse as pertaining to all marginalized voices and groups whose experiences have never been legitimized within this master narrative.

Baldwin experienced these racial distortions of his (and by extension, other blacks') humanity in the United States while seeking a sense of sense of authentic selfhood. In the beginning of "Nobody Knows My Name," he declared:

I left America because I doubted my ability to survive the fury of the color problem here. [...] I wanted to prevent myself from becoming *merely* a Negro; or even, merely a Negro writer. I wanted to find out in what way the *specialness* of my experience could be made to connect me with other people instead of dividing me from them. (Baldwin 1998, 137)

Here I imagine Baldwin as a scriptor of human possibilities, seeking an expansive view of the human capacity to relate and connect with others without being restricted by problematic racial constructs. With refreshing candor, he targeted white supremacy as a cultural value system that functioned to reduce and obscure his ability to connect with others (and with himself) on a more fundamental, existential level. In such a system, his blackness — its symbolic resonance and its tactile materiality — became a source of alienation and disconnection under the disconcerting white gaze.

As Baldwin also discovered, another form of this alienation would be felt beyond American borders in enlightened Europe. In the well known essay, "Stranger in the Village" (1953), Baldwin recounted his experiences living in a tiny Swiss village. Reflecting on what it meant to be a stranger thrown in a raced world that he had not created, Baldwin observed that the people of the village cannot be, from the point of view of power, strangers anywhere in the world. He wrote about the children's response to him as an exotic rarity as they shout *Neger! Neger!* in the streets, oblivious to his reaction (Baldwin, 1998). Notwithstanding the *saluts* and *bonsoirs* that Baldwin exchanged with his neighbors under the social convention of politeness, he saw in their eyes elements of paranoia and malevolence. In these encounters, Baldwin understood (or grasped) his "black" identity in personal and passionate terms. Notably, for Baldwin, this encounter with self was not a result of a disembodied, detached abstraction, but a deep involvement in the concreteness and full materiality of life. His experience in the Swiss village led him to reflect on the European roots of white racism and its later appearance in the United States:

> For this village brings home to me this fact: that there was a day, and not really a very distant day, when Americans were scarcely Americans at all but discontented Europeans, facing a great unconquered continent and strolling, say, into a marketplace and seeing black men for the first time. (Baldwin 1998, 124)

The very visibility of blackness that Baldwin alluded to — the sight of black skin — measures the importance of materiality in his racial discourse. This racialized discourse also provided the backdrop for Baldwin's bastard metaphor, alerting readers to his aspirations of acquiring ontological wholeness both for himself and others. Later, while reflecting on his sojourns in Europe and implicitly conjoining the singular with the collective, Baldwin inscribed a type of existence for black Americans that could at best be described, pathetically, as non-essential and marginal. In "Autobiographical Notes" from *Notes Of a Native Son,* Baldwin asserted:

> I know, in any case, that the most crucial time in my own development came when I was forced to recognize that I was a kind of bastard of the West; when I followed the line of my past I did not find myself in Europe but in Africa. And this meant that in some subtle way, in a really profound way, I brought to Shakespeare, Bach, Rembrandt, to the stones of Paris, to the cathedral at Chartres, and to the Empire State Building, a special attitude. These were not really my creations, they did not contain my history; I might search in them in vain forever for any reflection of myself. I was an interloper; this was not my heritage. (Baldwin 1998, 7–8)

The cultural resonance of Baldwin's bastard metaphor here is noteworthy. The cultural artifacts he encountered that purportedly symbolized the best of human aspirations, desires, hopes, and creativity did not reflect his contributions as an African American. With sobering awareness, his sense of illegitimacy is heightened when he realizes that in this Euro-American cultural lineage, he was essentially being confronted with prevailing configurations of the normative human: an ideology of whiteness.

Moreover, for Baldwin, experiencing oneself as a bastard evoked a sense of not knowing one's true, fuller identity. Indeed, black bastards in the U.S. are perpetually hidden from their truest selves when forced daily to wear a cloak of shame or inferiority that has been woven by a cultural legacy built on white supremacy. Equally important, in Baldwin's observations, American whites selfishly and ingeniously denied their culpability in creating this legacy of differentiation; in re-inventing — in more and more ingenious ways — the omnipresence of whiteness, white Americans intensified the alienating effects of problematic racial constructions. As he wrote, "The price that the white American paid for his ticket was to become white —: and, in the main, nothing more than that, or, as he was to insist, nothing less" (Baldwin 1985, xx).

With an emphasis on materiality and corporeality, Baldwin asserted again and again that black and white Americans are blood relatives — they shared the same biological origins. What his contemporaries often perceived as a racial problem essentially masked a more fundamental problem: forgetfulness of our common humanity. As he declared in *No Name in the Street* (1972), "The problem is rooted in the question of how one treats one's flesh and blood, especially one's children. The blacks are the despised and slaughtered children of the great Western house — nameless and unnamable bastards" (Baldwin 1998, 468).

With a critical awareness of experiencing oneself, one's people, one's culture as not quite genuine — as irregular, inferior, or of dubious origin — Baldwin spoke of cultivating a special attitude, [a] "special place in this scheme" (Baldwin 1998, 8). While not denying the reality of cultural and historical forces, Baldwin also declared that humans are always so much more than what our cultural markers claim for us. As he realized, "I had to claim my birthright. I am what time, circumstance, history, have made of me, certainly, but I am, also, much more than that. So are we all" (Baldwin 1998, 810).

These passages help underscore the ontological implications implicit in Baldwin's critical discourse. Claiming one's heritage is part of a more complex process of actualizing oneself as one relates to others, aspiring to achieve and experience one's humanity without falling prey to the damaging effects of a binary system that demarcates some humans as more, others as less. As he noted, the problematic question of African Americans' "humanity," and of their "rights as human being[s]" became such a burning question for several generations of Americans that it ultimately "became one of those used to divide the nation" (Baldwin 1998, 125).

However, for Baldwin, his — and all blacks' — heroic acts of self-actualization were not enough to address the great racial divide. Courageous acts by whites were crucial in helping to transform America; specifically, what was essentially needed was the honest admission by white Americans of their pivotal role in creating the current state of affairs in the America of his day: bastardizing blacks' existence there. In short, naming and foregoing the normativity of whiteness in America was tantamount. Historically, this meant whites admission of the systemic, widespread cultural violence perpetuated by the state in its construction and adoration of whiteness. White Americans must acknowledge, first and foremost, this shared history of blacks and whites. In *The Price of The Ticket,* Baldwin states:

> The record is there for all to read. It resounds all over the world. It might as well be written in the sky. One wishes that Americans — white Americans — would read, for their own sakes, this record and stop defending themselves against it. Only then will they be enabled to change their lives. The fact

that they have not yet been able to do this — to face their history, to change their lives — hideously menaces this country. Indeed, it menaces the entire world. (Baldwin 1985, 410–11)

According to Baldwin, the subjugated history perpetuated by white Americans was the key to their identity, as well as the triumph and justification of their history; furthermore, their material well-being depended on this continued subjugation. He asserts:

One may now see that the history, which is now indivisible from oneself, has been full of errors and excesses, but this is not the same thing as seeing that, for millions of people, this history — oneself — has been nothing but an intolerable yoke, a stinking prison, a shrieking grave. It is not so easy to see that, for millions of people, life itself depends on the speediest possible demolition of this history, even if this means the leveling, or the destruction of its heirs. (Baldwin 1985, 473)

To be heirs of history, in this context, is to construct and maintain the reality that one desires. Outsiders, or bastards, Baldwin suggests, are denied this very act of creating reality for oneself. In *No Name in the Street,* Baldwin asserted that white supremacy operates historically in prohibiting blacks in America (and the 'black' Algerians in France) from constructing their own freedom and choosing to become what they may desire. In other words, their experiences within the subjugated history of whiteness amounts to an essential lack of access to oneself: "The Algerian and I were both, alike, victims of this history, and I was still a part of Africa, even though I had been carried out of it nearly four hundred years before" (Baldwin 1998, 377).

The radical nature of materiality and historical positioning for Baldwin is notable here as he resists the pernicious and violence perpetrated by history in order to affirm unrecognized — or bastards' — accounts of history. Thus, an important insight of Baldwin, which I will emphasize in promoting my model of religious naturalism, is that humans do not transcend our variegated identities in the act of affirming our common humanity. Rather, we affirm our identities through a radically refigured conception of our humanity, which always includes historical specificity, diversity, and dynamic processing of becoming.

In other contexts, Baldwin also alluded to the formation of a bastard (outsider's) status that keeps blacks intimately identified with exile — or of not knowing home in the way that white Americans have created home in the U.S. — and thus of never feeling accepted, fully known, or even embraced by their white counterparts. He describes the tragic sense of forlornness that black Americans feel in experiencing a diaspora that never ends. As he describes it, "Later, in the midnight hour, the missing identity aches. One can neither assess nor overcome the storm of the middle passage. One is mysteriously shipwrecked forever, in the Great New World" (Baldwin 1985, xix).

Black Bastards, Desire, and Religious Entrapments

Baldwin's vision of a nobler view of humanity led him to indict the construction of whiteness in the United States, which both aided in demarcating and separating a common humanity that all shared and fostered myriad forms of alienation and hatred among various individuals and groups. In dismantling this edifice, he targeted a major cultural institution: religion, and specifically Christianity. Baldwin keenly recognized that key religious ideas functioned (either explicitly or implicitly) in a racist culture essentially to devalue black bodies as unworthy and inherently inferior to white ones, and they generated deeply embedded black self-loathing among many African Americans. In *To Crush a Serpent* (1987), one of his final published essays, Baldwin summed up a theme that he had addressed throughout many earlier ones: "Race and religion, it has been remarked, are fearfully entangled in the guts of this nation, so profoundly that to speak of the one is to conjure up the other. One cannot speak of sin without referring to blackness, and blackness stalks our history and our streets" (Baldwin 2010, 200).

Baldwin addressed the wider matrix of cultural meanings inherent in religious systems, showing how they both shape, and are shaped, by the behaviors of many black and white U.S. citizens. Within this context, the bastard metaphor was illuminating, as it helped Baldwin to underscore a truth that most wanted to ignore: white Americans denial of any familial kinship with blacks. As Baldwin observed in the interview with James Mossman, "The great dilemma of being a white American precisely is that they deny their only kinship" (Stanley and Pratt 1989, 50). He specifically targeted the hypocrisy of white Christians who, in an attempt to maintain their social order identity as white people, willfully denied their own moral connection (and biological kinship) to those of African descent, whom they continued to exploit.

In both dominant white Christian culture and the holiness tradition of his youth, which he saw as absorbing problematic ideological aspects of the former, Baldwin identified a root problem, manifest in various ways and on different levels: systematic vilification of blackness. He specifically targeted the symbol God as a reified marker that posited whiteness as representative of aesthetic and moral truths; equally important, it established whiteness as constitutive of normative humanity. Furthermore, whiteness was a social identity rooted in a god-complex, representing dominant culture's desperate avoidance of its own limitations as whites denied the beauty, value, and complex humanity of African Americans. He wrote at length about the depth of anti-blackness pervasive in American culture subtlety embedded in religious mechanisms. In *The Fire Next Time,* Baldwin observed:

> Negroes in this country — and Negroes do not, strictly or legally speaking, exist in any other — are taught really to despise themselves from the moment their eyes open on the world. This world is white and they are black. White people hold the power, which means that they are superior to blacks

(intrinsically, that is: God decreed it so), and the world has innumerable ways of making this difference known and felt and feared. (Baldwin 1998, 302)

In linking the notion of white supremacy with theistic belief and doctrinal certainty, Baldwin revealed why some cultural values entrenched in racial distortions appear as real, enduring, and authoritative truths. In the face of unrelenting racism and brutality, Baldwin thus saw structured religion as an obstacle to blacks' achieving authentic selfhood and integrity of being. In *To Crush a Serpent,* for example, Baldwin discussed the adverse psychological effects of those white Christian theological systems that invoked the curse of Ham to both justify slavery and devalue black subjectivities (Baldwin 2010: 196). The rabid antiblackness in such dangerous fabrications was alarming to Baldwin, who unmasked them as distortions of empirical truths.

Even more troubling for Baldwin were the insidious psychological effects on blacks of paying homage to the Christian deity. In commenting on the paradoxical nature of worship in the God-intoxicated holiness tradition of his youth, he observed: "But God — and I felt this even then, so long ago, on that tremendous floor, unwilling — is white. And if His love was so great, and if He loved all His children, why were we, the black, cast down so far?" (Baldwin 1998, 304–305). Although he acknowledged the black church (in all of its various structures) was often a haven and site of communal safety from blatant acts of racism, Baldwin also saw its complicity with white supremacy as blacks' harbored fear and hatred of their own bodies and those that looked like theirs. He perceived a form of self-hatred embedded in his tradition's ritualistic fervor and rites of purification where, ironically, distraught religious adherents often denied themselves the healing, love, and pleasure they were entitled to experience: "And the passion with which we loved the Lord was a measure of how deeply we feared and distrusted, and, in the end, hated almost all strangers, always, and avoided and despised ourselves" (Baldwin 1998, 310).

This awareness led Baldwin to another troubling insight: one unfortunate outcome of internalized anti-blackness was a lack of love in the black Church. In *The Fire Next Time,* Baldwin mused, "I really mean that there was no love in the church," adding that it was a mask for "hatred and self-hatred and despair" (Baldwin 1998, 309). Baldwin experienced and witnessed the degree to which this self-hatred — extraordinarily moralistic in tone — was a guise for advancing anti-body, anti-sexual, xenophobic, and homophobic sentiments. Such anti-love fostered a passivity and repression of all that he and others experienced as naturally good, and it required the relinquishing of one's individuality.

Amid the violent forms of alienation caused by problematic racial distinctions, Baldwin introduced a radical view of love. For Baldwin, love is a term that describes a state of being one affirms again and again in the process of choosing to enact one's authentic humanity:

> Love takes off the masks that we fear we cannot live without and know we cannot live within. I use the word "love" here not merely in the personal sense but as a state of being, or a state of grace — not in the infantile American sense of being made happy but in the tough universal sense of quest and daring and growth. (Baldwin 1998, 341)

With his usual flair and emotionality intensity, Baldwin conjoined the private and the public, the personal and the political, to describe a transformative embodied love that brings awareness of our common humanity. In "No Name in The Street," his eloquence is breathtaking when describing falling in love with another concrete, material human being — an experience that unhinges the entrapments of racial constructs:

> It began to pry open for me the trap of color, for people do not fall in love according to their color — this may come as news to noble pioneers and eloquent astronauts, to say nothing of most of the representatives of most of the American

states — and when lovers quarrel, as indeed they inevitably do, it is not the degree of their pigmentation that they are quarreling about, nor can lovers, on any level whatever, use color as a weapon. This means that one must accept one's nakedness. And nakedness has no color: this can come as news only to those who have never covered, or been covered by, another naked human being. (Baldwin 1998, 366)

Baldwin's embodied love described above evokes the Sartrean notion of intersubjectivity: Recognizing the humanity of the other before oneself confronts one's subjectivity in the most immediate way, both limiting and enabling what one could possibly choose in any given context. This intimate encounter of knowing and being known by another brings with it a new awareness of seeing others differently and experiencing one's humanity as both free and bound. As Baldwin stated, an individual is both stronger and more vulnerable, both free and bound: "Free, paradoxically, because, now, you have a home — your lover's arms. And bound: to that mystery, precisely, a bondage which liberates you into something of the glory and suffering of the world" (Baldwin 1989, 366).

The embodied love Baldwin evoked also imbued traditional religious terms with new fresh, expanded meanings. His radical view of love was "something active, more like a fire, like a wind," not an empty abstraction describing a passive stance before some authorial figure outside of oneself (Stanley and Pratt 1998, 48). Here, we see Baldwin rejecting the traditional other-worldly eschatological discourse of fear and damnation featured in holiness traditions, and replacing it with an emphasis on the concrete dynamics of living here and now. Likewise, salvation is that which we must do to save each other; for Baldwin, the most crucial aspect of salvation is its rootedness in human actions and efforts. The contingencies of life and concreteness of human experiences require redemptive actions from humans themselves. In "To Crush a Serpent" Baldwin asserted that salvation does not divide, but conjoins, so that "one sees oneself in others and others in oneself. It is not the exclusive property of any dogma, creed, or church. It keeps the channel open between oneself and however one wishes to name That which is greater than oneself" (Baldwin 2010, 203).

Baldwin believed embracing embodied love could result in a vital flourishing for all North Americans. He reiterated this theme in a speech he gave in San Francisco in October of 1960. Addressing the writer's role in American life, Baldwin emphasized and articulated a moral vision that celebrates the potential of newly formed human relationships to create and sustain new possibilities for Americans. In his thinking, humans displace the traditional God and enact transformation in their lives, redeeming themselves from impoverished, erroneous views of their shared humanity. For example, after insisting on necessary changes to the dominant configuration of raced living in America, Baldwin ended the speech with the following words about the U.S.:

> It will not be transformed by an act of God, but by all of us, by you and me. I don't believe any longer that we can afford to say that it is entirely out of our hands. We made the world we're living in and we have to make it over. (Baldwin 1992, 154)

In Baldwin's hands, traditional African-American religiosity is destabilized and uprooted from a metaphysical system that pits a supernatural deity over and against sinful humans. He displaced traditional supernaturalism, exchanging the external deity beyond nature for the power of love expressed in embodied, material human relationships. In short, for Baldwin, humans save each other. As D. Quentin Miller suggested, one can see Baldwin moving from the ultimate expression of external authority — God — to the broader community collectively and individually (Miller 2000, 3).

Furthermore, the fuller expression of Baldwin's form of communal ontology recognized a common humanity constitutive of our biotic materiality on which various identity markers are couched and binary oppositions attached. As he emphatically stated at one point: "It is so simple a fact and one that is so hard, apparently, to grasp: *Whoever debases others is debasing himself*" (Baldwin 1998, 334). Here, Baldwin anticipated the basic thrust of my religious naturalism, which emphasizes the deep genetic homology structuring all life forms — what I describe as humans' interconnectedness with each other and with all natural organisms.

Our Common Humanity: Emergence of an African-American Religious Naturalism

An African-American religious naturalism emerges out of a critical awareness that religiosity is not necessarily centered in any specific tradition. Rather, it can be a mode of reflecting on, experiencing, and envisioning one's relationality with all that is. Here, I evoke the views of Peter Van Ness, who wrote eloquently of the spiritual dimension of life "as the embodied task of realizing one's truest self in the context of reality apprehended as a cosmic totality. It is the quest for attaining an optimal relationship between what one truly is and everything that is" (Van Ness 1996, 5). Consequently, a fuller emergence of this African-American religious naturalism is possible if, and only if, we continue to keep our focus on artful, material human organisms, or on the efforts of relational humans. Within the context of African-American life and culture, this means that any truths we are ever going to discover, and any meaning in life we will uncover, are revealed to us through our own efforts as natural beings. This religious view expressly rejects any suggestion of the supernatural — there is nothing that transcends the natural world. Donald Crosby provided an elegant summary of the prominent status of nature in religious naturalism:

> Nature requires no explanation beyond itself. It always has existed and always will exist in some shape or form. Its constituents, principles, laws, and relations are the sole reality. This reality takes on new traits and possibilities as it evolves inexorably through time. Human beings are integral parts

of nature, and they are natural beings through and through. They, like all living beings, are outcomes of biological evolution. They are embodied beings whose mental or spiritual aspect is not something separate from their bodies but a function of their bodily nature. There is no realm of the supernatural and no supernatural being or beings residing in such a realm. (Cosby 2008, ix–x)

Nature itself becomes a focal point for assessing our human desires, dreams, and possibilities — for assessing what can emerge from the past. Fifty years removed from Baldwin's nomadic sensibilities and his emphasis on materiality and embodied desire, I envision a religious naturalism that requires us to take seriously the idea of our humanity as an achievement, not a given. More specifically, this emergent religious naturalism compels African Americans to reflect meaningfully on the emergence of matter (and especially life) from the Big Bang forward, promoting an understanding of myriad nature as complex processes of becoming. Its theoretical appeal is the fundamental conception of humans as natural processes intrinsically connected to other natural processes. This insight helps to blur the arbitrary ontological lines that human animals have erected between other species and natural processes and us.

With Loyal Rue, I endorse a portrayal of human beings as star-born, earth-formed creatures endowed by evolutionary processes to seek reproductive fitness under the guidance of biological, psychological, and cultural systems that have been selected for their utility in mediating adaptive behaviors (Rue 2005, 77). Humans maximize their chances for reproductive fitness by managing the complexity of these systems in ways that are conducive to the simultaneous achievement of personal wholeness and social coherence. Rue wrote:

The meaning of human life should be expressed in terms of how our particular species pursues the ultimate telos of reproductive fitness. Like every other species, we seek the ultimate biological goal according to our peculiar nature. That is, by pursuing the many teloi that are internal to our behavior mediation systems, whether these teloi are built into the system by genetic means or incorporated into them by symbolic means. For humans there are many immediate teloi, including the biological goals inherent in our drive systems, the psychological goals implicit in our emotional and cognitive systems, and the social goals we imbibe through our symbolic systems. Human life is about whatever these goals are about. (Rue 2005, 75)

Appreciating human life as one distinct biotic form emerging from, and participating in, a series of evolutionary processes that constitute the diversity of life has monumental implications for African-American culture. Here, the scientific epic becomes the starting point for positing an African-American religious humanism constituted by a central tenet: humans are relational processes of nature; in short, we are nature made aware of itself. In declaring such, I contend that our *humanity* is not a given, but rather an achievement.

Consider that from a strictly biological perspective, humans are organisms that have slowly evolved by a process of natural selection from earlier primates. From one generation to another, the species that is alive now has gradually adapted to changing environments so that it could continue to survive. Our animality, from this perspective, is living under the influence of genes, instincts, and emotions with the prime directive to survive and procreate. Yet, this minimalist approach fails to consider what a few cognitive scientists and most philosophers, humanists, and religionists tend to accentuate: our own personal experience of what it is like to be an experiencing human being. Becoming human, or actualizing ourselves as human beings, in this sense, emerges out of an awareness and desire to be more than a conglomeration of pulsating cells. It is suggesting that our humanity is not reducible to organizational patterns or processes dominated by brain structures, nor do DNA, diet, behavior, and the environment solely structure it. Human animals become human destinies when we posit fundamental questions of value, meaning, and purpose to our existence. Our coming to be human destinies is structured by a crucial question: How do we come to terms with life? (White 2016, 32–33).

In this African-American religious view, sacrality is a specific affirmation and appreciation of that which is fundamentally important in life or that which is ultimately valued: relational Nature. Humans are interconnected parts of Nature, and our sacrality is a given part of Nature's richness, spectacular complexity, and beauty. Notwithstanding the diverse cultural and individual approaches of articulating this truth, there is for me, quite simply, the sacrality of human deep interconnectedness with all that is. Finding meaning and value in our lives within the natural order presupposes our fundamental interconnectedness. We can claim and become our humanity in seeking and finding community with others — and with otherness. This is a simple value that religious discourse has advanced and reiterated again and again. As Ursula Goodenough observed:

> We have throughout the ages sought connection with higher powers in the sky or beneath the earth, or with ancestors in some other realm. We have also sought, and found, religious fellowship with one another. And now we realize that we are connected to all creatures. Not just in food chains or ecological equilibria. We share a common ancestor. We share genes for receptors and cell cycles and signal-transduction cascades. We share evolutionary constraints and possibilities. We are connected all the way down. (Goodenough 1998, 75)

The basic conception of the human as an emergent, interconnected life form amid spectacular biotic diversity has far-reaching ethical implications within the context of African-American culture. First, it contributes to an intellectual legacy that has attempted to overcome the deficient conceptions of our humanity ensnared in problematic racial constructions. African-American religious naturalism presupposes human beings as biotic forms emerging from evolutionary processes sharing a deep homology with other sentient beings and also valuing such connections. Accordingly, it challenges racially constructed views that have persistently placed blacks outside of the circle of humanity.

Second, this model of African American rejects a view of our humanity solely as an individualistic phenomenon — some type of communal ontology is implied. A crucial lesson here is that notwithstanding the cultural and national differences and specificities we construct, humans are all genetically connected and part of a greater whole — any harm done to another human is essentially harm done to ourselves. We are essentially celebrating a relational self that can resist solipsistic tendencies and egoistic impulses: there is no isolated self who stands over against the fields of interaction. Put another way, there is no private self or final line between interiority and exteriority — we always include the other (even if by acting to exclude it). The self is constitutionally relational and inevitably entangled in temporal becoming.

Finally, this African-American religious naturalism provides the impetus and vision for continued social justice action in the twenty-first century. With its emphasis on deep connectivity — with oneself, family, larger human community, local and global ecosystems, and the universe — this religious naturalism seeks a transformed existence. Religiously, this implies love, and love implies concern for the well being of the beloved. African-American religious naturalism reinforces perennial, expansive perspectives from the wisdom traditions that adamantly promote kindness, empathy, and compassion for all natural processes, including human ones. With the capacity to influence each other and other natural processes, humans have a responsibility to act in ways that promote the flourishing of all life, and to urge other humans that may be less inclined to acknowledge our interconnectedness to do the same. Any inkling of white supremacy, or sense of cultural superiority of any ilk, is antithetical to this natural view; these eschewed cultural constructions are forced impositions on the wholeness of natural interrelatedness and deep homology that evolution has wrought (White 2016, 34).

Baldwin's America: From Bastards to Freaks

With its conception of human animals as value-laden organisms, African-American religious naturalism encourages us to challenge the most viral constructions of "isms" rooted in problematic self-other differentiations. Inspired by Baldwin's concept of embodied love, this religiosity resists normalizing discourses (often disguised as moral truths) that thwart human desire to connect with and love others. In short, it engages in queer resistance. Here I return again to Baldwin to underscore this point. In doing so, I evoke Melvin Dixon's extended use of the notion of *lieux de mémoire* (sites of memory) to augment the importance of Baldwin's work for inaugurating a black queer sensibility that challenged traditional race-centered discourses in African-American critical writing (Dixon 2006). I also follow the lead of Michael L. Cobb and others, who remind us of the ways in which Baldwin illuminated the complicated intersections of queerness, blackness, and religious rhetoric (Cobb and Michael 2001). In this brief discussion, I focus on his essays and interviews rather than influential fictional works, which also reflect these perspectives.

Because Baldwin did not fit standard heterosexual norms, people sought to label him. As he imagined a space to live authentically, Baldwin found certain categories reductive and impoverishing, failing to capture the full experience of human connection he sought. His queer sensibilities recognized that these labels were not merely handy descriptions in a culture that he had not helped to design; rather, they conveyed implicit moral and ontological meanings and were used to restrict his humanity and distort his nomadic desiring. During an interview with journalist James Mossman and Colin MacInnes in 1965, Baldwin asserted:

[T]hose terms, homosexual, bisexual, heterosexual are 20th-century terms which, for me, really have very little meaning. I've never, myself, in watching myself and watching other people, watching life, been able to discern exactly where the

> barriers were. Life being what life is, and passion being what passion is. (Stanley and Pratt 1989, 54)

In keeping with my robust reading of Baldwin, I see this response as an enactment of queer resistance. Baldwin refused to see his desire to connect intimately with another male as an example of a "homosexual" summation. He recognized that categories of sexual identity are often used to demarcate and evaluate the wide range of erotic desire along a continuum, implying a range from the normative to the illegitimate. Moreover, Baldwin saw that "distrust of the affections and of the flesh […] [is] revealed most grotesquely in what we call the sexual deviants, the sexual minorities, who are really simply the most vivid victims of our system of mortification of the flesh" (Stanley and Pratt 1989, 55).

In a 1985 essay titled "Here Be Dragons" (also published as "Freaks and the American Ideal of Manhood"), Baldwin also made fruitful connections among race, erotic-desiring beings, and nationalistic mythology. He observed that U.S. expressions of sexuality were rooted in an American ideal of masculinity, which perpetuate problematic binary differentiations: "good guys and bad guys, punks and studs, tough guys and softies, butch and faggot, black and white" (Baldwin 1998, 815). Drawing on his personal experiences as a young black male exploring desire in Greenwich Village, Baldwin described lonely, alienating encounters with other males (often white or of another ethnicity) who both expressed desire for him as well as self-revulsion in desiring a black queer male. He also noted the virtual absence of black women in the Village when describing a few sexual encounters with white women whom he feared brought to their sexual encounters the desire to "civilize you into becoming an appendage" or with the individual who desired "a black boy to sleep with because she wanted to humiliate her parents" (Baldwin 1998, 824).

In Baldwin's nomenclature of desire, he became a freak. Here, a key insight of his analysis is that freaks represent an epistemic marker that conjoins race, gender, and sexuality in U.S. culture. Freaks are deviant individuals who do not conform to the ideal

standards of sexuality and normative configurations of masculine identity within a racist, homophobic culture. Baldwin
observed: "Freaks are called freaks and are treated as they are
treated — in the main, abominably — because they are human
beings who cause to echo, deep within us, our most profound
terrors and desires" (Baldwin 1998, 828). Accordingly, freaks un-
cloak a horrific and terrifying truth about purportedly "normal"
people, providing insight into the dangers, violence, and weak-
nesses endemic to the American ideal of masculinity. As such,
freaks remain outliers, sharing with bastards an illegitimacy that
keeps the cultural myth intact.

As a site of memory, Baldwin's case is illuminative. Earlier
he had critiqued the dangers of establishing the pure white god
as the ontological grounding for an inferior humanity in which
blacks represented the most depraved case. Here, in a parallel
move, we see Baldwin exposing another sacrosanct truth based
on whiteness: an ontological ordering that established white
male heterosexuality the norm for ascertaining and evaluating
other expressions of desire. Confronting this standard, Baldwin
exposed a national psyche enshrouded in a fear of materiality, femininity, and blackness. For Baldwin, black gay, effemi-
nate men are archetypes of this triple threat — they fascinate as
phantasms and yet are reviled as actual humans. While limited
in its lack of serious attention to female bodies, lesbian desires,
or even complex configurations of femininity, Baldwin's insights
are nonetheless helpful and anticipate later queer interventions
and orientations.

With rapt attention to multiplicities and differences in desire
and embodied love, Baldwin problematized the constitutions
of gender and sexual identities as binary, separated, and fixed
categories. He also alerted us to the dangers of emplacing what
is fluid and porous with normalizing discourses. Going beyond
a vision of our humanity dictated by compulsory heterosexuality, he ends this absorbing essay with an image of an androgy-
nous humanity where inter-related, inter-connected sexual, racial and gendered beings belong to each other. As he declared:
"[E]ach of us, helplessly and forever, contains the other — male

47

in female, female in male, white in black, and black in white. We are a part of each other" (Baldwin 1998, 828).

Polyamorous Bastards: Becoming Our Humanity

Inspired by Baldwin's creative reach, my trajectory of African-American religious naturalism promotes a black queer critical consciousness that resists regimes of the normal. In this final section, I elaborate on this point, utilizing Claudia Schippert's work in queer theory and religion to underscore African-American religious naturalism as an instance of queer religiosity. In "Implications of Queer Theory for the Study of Religion and Gender: Entering the Third Decade," Schippert observed that queer theoretical analysis itself is an emergent discourse that continually shifts and translates in diverse geographic-cultural configurations (Schippert 2011). Furthermore, within the context of religious scholarship and studies, queer theory continues to expand its theoretical applicability and usefulness. For Schippert, then, queering religion has something to do with expanding the sphere and proper object of study in religion. This is what Schippert suggested with the term 'undisciplined' religion:

> When approaching religion queerly then, we can no longer simply 'add' queer identities to an 'inclusive' liberationist agenda. [...] The implications of the challenges and rethinking of the field of religion indicate that what is being studied as the discipline of religion is shifting focus on previously excluded topics. Studying religion queerly can be, and perhaps will need to be, (more) undisciplined. (Schippert 2011, 74)

The emergent African-American religious naturalism that I have sketched in this essay contributes to this undisciplined space. As a trajectory of religiosity in African-American culture, it destabilizes traditional religious methods that purport to establish humanity's desires of actualization on metaphysical views of a superior deity; this religiosity also problematizes the notion that religious ideas and ethical practices are necessarily grounded in transcendental ideals. Rather, it honors the complex ways value-laden human animals attempt to enact our desire for others, fulfilling emotional, physical, and psychological needs. Rejecting traditional onto-theological claims of reality as the source of our being, this religious perspective celebrates value-laden organisms fundamentally coming to terms with life, or making sense of their existence, in relationship with others. Compelled by the evolutionary epic, this queer African-American religious naturalism offers an expanded view of humans as intrinsically relational, natural organisms and vital centers of value — or humans as lovers of life, motivated by a desire for goodness and connection with all that is.

Schippert also noted that queer religiosity has placed much more focus on transnational and diasporic identities, including a plethora of voices, identities, bodies, and cultural ways of being both queer and religious. Here, queer theorists are mindful of addressing "identities, community and consumption practices, and the workings of kinship and family practices in more complex configurations. No longer is the white, gay, Western (Christian/secular) man the assumed author, audience, or object of study within queer theoretical texts" (Schippert 2011, 75). The queer African-American religious perspective I endorse here supports this task. With an expansive view of our common humanity, it compels us to keep in focus the desires of marginalized, often forgotten humans — polyamorous bastards — who resist substantive ontologies and onto-theological loyalties. Inspired by Baldwin, Audre Lorde, Bayard Rustin, and countless other nameless bastards and freaks who dared to humanize their desire, it accentuates the pleasurable "roaming" of a queer love that celebrates humans' radical relationality with each other and, I emphasize, with other natural processes. However, unlike the lonely repressed males sketched by Baldwin in "Here Be Freaks," polyamorous bastards wander with bold audacity, cherishing all forms of materiality.

Evoking Baldwin's sense of the illegitimacy shared by bastards and freaks, queer African-American religious naturalism also assumes a self-critical stance against normativity. This point needs a bit of clarification in light of Schippert's discussion of the new homonormativity in Lisa Duggan's analysis of the sexual politics of neoliberal conservatism. As a strain of conservative moralism, Duggan argued, homonormativity's aim is in establishing the 'normality' of the 'good' and responsible outsider subject, along similar lines used in defining the heteronormative subject (Schippert 2011, 77). Within communities of color already marginalized by the edifice of white supremacy, this general idea serves as a helpful reminder when establishing our participation in an expansive humanity. We should be careful not to erect new norms and classifications that further vilify perceivable deviant "others," specifically in gendered, racialized, class-marked, or sexual terms. Furthermore, as I have argued elsewhere, any conceivable notion of our common humanity will be ontologically enmeshed and entangled with other forms of natural life. In keeping with the tenets of religious naturalism, we consistently resist the aims of traditional humanism that have posited humans outside of myriad nature and eclipsed the interrelatedness of all natural processes.

Those of us inspired by this queer African-American religious naturalism recognize the inclination in humans to institutionalize our reified constructions as normative views of truth or standards of practice. Whatever principles we deem sacred or effective in shaping our desires can never be divorced from cultural constructions, social/political contexts, and institutionalizing processes. However, in seeking to reorder "issues concerning identities, nationalism, communities, and material practices," we remain open to newer forms of becoming (Schippert 2011, 76). In short, achieving our humanity remains an ongoing, critical task — we never arrive. The queer religiosity I outline here accentuates this point. Furthermore, employing the metaphors of pores (openings), it accentuates the fluidity of purportedly fixed (or given) differences. Here, queer religiosity seeks to illuminate the porous nature of fixed markers that purport to reveal our identities (e.g., race, sexuality, and gender), to emplace our bodies (e.g., institutions, buildings, nations, and borders), and to specify our locations (e.g., cultural, geographic, social-economic).

Finally, this emerging African-American religious natural-ism evokes Baldwin's concept of redemptive embodied love, which he introduced to inspire and challenge his contempo-raries to conceive and hope beyond what seemed immediate and obvious. In the contemporary era, queer religious prac-tice finds all Americans confronting and rejecting ideologies that perpetually bifurcate our humanity, and instill a shameful sense of inferiority and unworthiness in some and a false sense of superiority in others. Focusing upon the variegated beauty that evolution has wrought, we celebrate our differences even while honoring our common humanity. Equally important, we unhinge problematic stigmas of unnaturalness, illegitimacy, or even freakishness from our engagement with others as we ex-plore nomadic human desire.

Here, Baldwin's prophetic words in *The Price of the Ticket* are apropos: "Go back to where you started, or as far back as you can, examine all of it, travel your road again and tell the truth about it. Sing or shout or testify or keep it to yourself: but *know whence you came* (Baldwin 1998, 841).

References

Baldwin, James. 1985. *The Price of the Ticket: Collected Non-Fiction, 1948–1985*. New York: St. Martin's Press

———. 2010. *The Cross of Redemption: Uncollected Writings*. New York: Vintage.

———. 1998. *Baldwin: Collected Essays*. Edited by Toni Morrison. New York: The Library of America.

———. 1992. "Notes for a Hypothetical Novel." In *Nobody Knows My Name*. New York: Vintage.

———, James Mossman, and Colin MacInnes. 1965. "Race, Hate, Sex, and Colour: A Conversation." *Encounter* 25. 55–60.

Cobb, Michael. 2001. "Pulptic Publicity: James Baldwin and the Queer Uses of Religious Words." *Journal of Gay and Lesbian Studies* 7.2. 285–312.

Crosby, Donald. 2008. *Living with Ambiguity: Religious Naturalism and the Menace of Evil*. Albany: SUNY Press.

Douglass, Frederick. 2000. *Frederick Douglass: Selected Speeches and Writings*. Edited by Philip S. Foner and Yuval Taylor. Chicago: Chicago Review Press.

Goodenough, Ursula. 1998. *The Sacred Depths of Nature*. New York: Oxford University Press.

Kaplan, Cora and Bill Schwartz. 2011. *James Baldwin: America and Beyond*. Ann Arbor: The University of Michigan Press.

Miller, D. Quentin, ed. 2000. *Re-viewing James Baldwin: Things Not Seen*. Philadelphia: Temple University Press.

Rue, Loyal. 2005. *Religion Is Not About God*. Piscataway: Rutgers University Press.

Schippert, Claudia. 2011. "Implications of Queer Theory for the Study of Religion and Gender: Entering the Third Decade." *Religion and Gender* 1.1. 66–84.

Standley, Fred and Louis H. Pratt. 1989. *Conversations with James Baldwin*. Jackson: University Press of Mississippi.

Warner, Michael. 1993. "Introduction." In M. Warner, ed. *Fear of a Queer Planet: Queer Politics and Social Theory*. Minneapolis: University of Minnesota Press. vii–xxxi

Van Ness, Peter H. 1996. *Spirituality and the Secular Quest.* New York: Crossroad.

West, Cornel. 1982. *Prophesy Deliverance! An Afro-American Revolutionary Christianity.* Philadelphia: Westminster Press.

White, Carol W. 2016. *Black Lives and Sacred Humanity: Toward an African American Religious Naturalism.* New York: Fordham University Press.

CHAPTER 2

Irreverent Theology:
On the Queer Ecology of Creation

Jacob J. Erickson

> *Nature is infinitely scandalous!*
> — Isabella Rossellini

> *All this would entail, in the larger scheme of things,*
> *an irreverent turn in ecocriticism…*
> — Nicole Seymour

Scandalizing Nature and God

"How did Noah do it?" the Italian-American actress Isabella Rossellini asks inquisitively. She is dressed in black, stands in front of a similar black background, and holds in her right hand a yellow umbrella. "How did he manage to organize all animals," she asks *you,* "into couples?"[1] Rossellini poses this question in the course of a series of hilarious and provocative short films produced for the Sundance Channel on the theme of *Green Porno.* In the course of those films, she artistically explores the complexities of animal sex, performing a variety of animal spe-

---

1   Isabella Rossellini's video "Seduce Me — Noah's Ark" can be found at: http://www.youtube.com/watch?v=3WBr7aVADtU.

cies and exploring their sexual quirks, oddities, and pleasures. As she describes the series in the book inspired by her project, "I imagine myself as a particular animal and make love as that animal would. Each film is scientifically accurate; nature is infinitely scandalous" (Rossellini 2009).

Infinitely scandalous nature is precisely the odd focus of Rossellini's peculiar film about the biblical story of Noah. She observes that God calls pairs of animals into Noah's ark precisely to sexually reproduce, to repopulate the earth, to "be fruitful and multiply" after the mythic flood. But, as Rossellini goes on to show, such a task is biologically fraught.

The scene's imagination expands: a large pop-up book *Holy Bible* opens and out emerges the biblical story. A cloud, rain, and lightning appear above the wooden ark while God's arm — Rossellini's arm with hair drawn in marker all over — scrutinizes the animals entering the ark two by two.[2] First, elephants climb the boarding ramp — genitals prominently on display, male and female. Following the elephants, however, is a lone earthworm, and the situation gets complicated:

"You!" God accuses. "Why are you alone?"

"I'm an earthworm. I am an hermaphrodite." Rossellini replies, in the guise of her earthwormed costume. "I'm both male and female. To reproduce, I can mate with another hermaphrodite, or I can segment my body and clone myself."

The human Rossellini reappears, asking quizzically, "What did Noah do with hermaphrodite animals? What did Noah do with transsexual animals?"

---

2   The flood narrative in Genesis is, of course, a complicated text in and of itself — woven together strands of the Yahwist and Priestly creation narratives. Rossellini's treatment of the Noah story misses a number of crucial details of the actual story — most that it is commonly held that in the Priestly version of the story two of every kind of animal are taken onto the ark, whereas in Yahwist version of the story, seven pairs of all clean animals and a pair of all unclean animals are taken. The intertextual difference is quite often overlooked, though this difference in the text would little change the reality of Rossellini's argument. See Genesis 6–11 for the flood story.

And the piece spirals on — hermaphrodite animals, animals that change sex, animals that transition sex and sexuality, parthenogenetic species that reproduce asexually all appear on the boarding plank up to Noah's ark, making complicated God's command that only "one male and one female" be allowed on the ark.

The short film concludes with a biological provocation that extends beyond the scope of the biblical myth she reenacts. Rossellini asks, "How did Noah do it — hermaphrodite, transvestites, transgender, transsexuals, polygamy, monogamy, homosexual, bisexual — how could it all be heterosexual?" And the sound of rain pours on...

"How could it all be heterosexual?" The question seems innocuous enough, but the inquiry opens a veritable can of hermaphroditic worms. On the surface level the question begins to subvert the literal logics of the religious narrative. Taken on its own terms, the story of Noah's flood is an impossible one, mythic in its telling, upended by the biological facts of life. That upending, for Rossellini, also seems to attempt an upending of the social and theological forces that often read biblical texts in an overtly literalistic manner. Such theological viewpoints often contribute to a rhetoric celebrating and assuming heterosexual life and relationships as norm. Those theological viewpoints often scapegoat queer lives by calling them deviant. By lifting up biological oddities in a strange kind of midrashic retelling of the flood story, Rossellini's questions subtly challenge the assumptions of broader heterosexist theologies and hermeneutics.

The film also serves to subvert our cultural assumptions about everyday biology. Animal life is not divided into heterosexual pairs, and the diversity of animal sex and sexuality multiplies in strange and surprising ways. What biologists may take for granted about the queer sexual pleasures and reproductive lives of the animal kingdom, viewers are suddenly reminded of or confronted by. Not only are preconceptions of religious storytelling to be rethought, but also Rossellini exposes heterosexist assumptions projected onto nonhuman life through an ecological parade of animal sex and sexualities.

At this point, we might deduce yet another subversion. If neither assumptions of scripture nor projections of biology fully encapsulate actual life, then what about the question implicates human beings? Not all of human reality — yours, mine — is heterosexual, despite the assumptions of heterosexism structuring various oppressive regimes. The analogy is such — if animals, in their sexual and biological diversity, are more complex than a certain reading of the biblical text indicates, might not the sexuality of human animals be more complex as well? Might human beings themselves corporealize a diversity of sexes, sexualities, genders, and relationships?

Rossellini's art is playfully irreverent of theological and biological imagination; indeed its irreverent of human imaginings of the ecological world. Her performances expose the viewer's assumptions about what constitutes theological culture, what constitutes what is "natural," and further exposes how deeply implicated culture and nature are together. Her art and the questions her art raises makes it possible for the viewer to reconceive their ecological world, their religious expectations, or their understanding of what it means to be a human being all together. The theological, the erotic, and the human all entangle one another in assumptions shaping attentiveness and negligence of actual planetary life. If animal sexuality (if we can use that phrase at all) is far more complex than is often assumed, what does that mean for theological reflection, ecological relationships, or human life and responsibility for nonhuman life?

It's true, talking about "queer ecology" might conjure up strange rumors of gay penguins or evoke bestial accusations against queer communities. But for the last few decades an emerging theoretical conversation between environmental ethics and queer theory — like Rossellini's art — has been stirring up new perspectives on the constructed boundaries of nature and culture, animality and humanity, ecological responsibility and environmental degradation. Recent volumes entitled *Queering the Non/Human* and *Queer Ecologies* examine everything from biophilia to *Brokeback Mountain,* eros to starfish, and reproduction to bunny rabbits (with the latter not being a very large leap).[3] As Timothy Morton summarizes in his influential piece, "Ecology and queer theory are intimate. It's not that ecological thinking would benefit from an injection of queer theory from the outside. It's that, fully and properly, ecology is queer theory and queer theory is ecology: queer ecology" (Morton 2010, 281).

Scholars of religion, theologians and ethicists, both antici-pated and followed this turn in the nineties by incorporating religious perspectives with lesbian and gay liberation, queer theory and ecological ethics. A number of ecofeminists, theolo-gians like J. Michael Clark, and ethicists like Daniel T. Spencer provided insightful analyses of the twin ghettoization of LGTBQ voices and the earth. They point towards, as Spencer describes, the "self-contradictory positions of condemning lesbians and gay men for being both 'unnatural' (where natural sexuality is read as procreative heterosexuality) and 'too close to nature' in the sense of homosexual behavior being 'lower' or 'animal-istic' and outside the boundaries of acceptable human culture" (Spencer 1996, 80–81). In this way, these scholars focused on the fraught eco-social and material dimensions of queer and eco-logical voices.

My own goal in this chapter seeks to further this remark-able interdisciplinary conversation in an odd theological key by engaging the recent work of feminist philosopher of science, Karen Barad. Barad's writing *is* key, I think, for mutually-en-hancing and collaborating the insights of queer theory, philoso-phies of science, and ecology. Particularly, I stage an encounter between Barad's concept of "posthumanist performativity" and the sixteenth-century reformer and monk Martin Luther's pe-

---

3   For earlier attempts at a queer ecotheology, see the multiple trends of eco-feminism and ecowomanism, as well as: Clark 1993; Spencer 1996. Along-side the work of Clark or Spencer, see the growing bodies of queer eco-logical literature (the following are listed chronologically): Gaard 1997; the work of the journal *Undercurrents*; Stein 2004; Barad 2007; Giffney and Hird 2008; Alaimo 2010; Morton 2010; Mortimer-Sandilands and Erickson 2010; Halberstam 2011; Johnson 2011; Azzarello 2012; Boer 2012; Chen 2012; Roughgarden 2013; Seymour 2013; Ahmed 2014; the chapter on Walt Whit-man in Keller 2015; and Keller and Rubenstein 2017.

culiar understanding of the incarnation of Spirit in Creation. I do so to begin to construct a queer ecotheology where Luther's passion for incarnation, critically reimagined with Barad's work, offers the potential for a queer incarnation of divinity where that divinity is caught up — even plays several roles — in the performative indeterminacy of the earth and of the cosmos. In the irreverent slippage of God and earth, "creation" signals a divinely queer ecology.[4]

The Irreverent Collaborations of Queer Ecology

Rossellini's short film is just a finite glimpse into what is possible in the infinitely scandalous interrelations of theology, ecology, and sexuality. What follows in my theological writing is a fragile, playful, expansive hope for theology that wishes to take our contemporary planetary crises seriously in their depths of life and death. What follows is a fragile, playful hope that queer bodies, queer failures and pleasures, and queer play and hope might offer some distinctive imagination to ecological theologies as they attempt to think on a dying planet — at least a planet dying, for the first time, at the hands of human beings. What follows is nothing more than a creative hunch, a speculative possibility of flesh. What follows is nothing more than a playful caress of theology. My flirtation is that ecological theology is, or can be, a poetry and practice of irreverent criticism, of irreverence to conceptual realities overwhelmed by ecological crises.

In arguing for *theological* irreverence, I am constructively rallying to and riffing off of ecocritic Nicole Seymour's call for what she calls an "irreverent ecocriticism," a kind of criticism "whose inquiries are absurd, perverse, humorous in character, and/or focused on the absurd, perverse, and humorous as they arise in relationship to ecology and representations thereof" (Seymour 2012, 57). Given the state of environmental collapse, the continuous reports of ecological devastation, and multiply-

---

4   I use the terminology of "earth" here to signify not any kind of foundationalist ground, but a kind of nominalization of dynamic planetarity.

ing effects of global warming, she asks how we might continue in our ecological work. How might we go forward given the deep helplessness and hopelessness of our current milieu?

Drawing on contemporary, poststructuralist thought and queer ecology, Seymour argues for an irreverent turn that "would allow us to address and grapple with [...] those emotional and conceptual pressures we face" (Seymour 2012, 61). As she notes, there's "something laughable, even hilarious, about the collective position of the ecocritic in the face of ongoing environmental devastation. Rather than ignore that hilarity," she continues, "I want us to talk about it" (Seymour 2012, 68). To talk about that hilarity, Seymour argues, focuses on our awkward dispositions, affects, silly constructions, ideas, and low culture that may, in fact, offer political ways of feeling out the undeniable ambiguity and uncertainty of the current moment. Irreverence might be a way of materially navigating the difficult absurdities of our current moment while still committing ourselves to the political and ethical possibilities ecocritical writing often (absurdly) desires.

Still, irreverence seems innocuous, too, at first. The phrase sounds like I'm simply not taking my theological work seriously enough. I may be coyly joking about God, giggling in church, or scandalizing theological language. But, perhaps, you may assume that by irreverence I'm intentionally trying to destroy or disrespect theology or practices of faith (only certain kinds). Disrespect is hardly my intention, though I most certainly flirt with such danger. In point of fact, my imagination is seduced by an irreverent faith and an irreverent reflection of faith.

Even more, however, my own desire for an irreverent ecocriticism is aimed at nothing less than the most revered: "Nature" and "God."[5] Two ontotheological concepts — two sovereign subjects imagined and imaged in the Modern era — utterly distant

---

5   The complication here, of course, is that the celebration of the concept of "Nature" as uncivilized land, empty land, and ordered land instigated a level of ecological degradation never before seen on the face of the earth — so much so that we now find ourselves in a planet irrevocably shaped by the plunder, violence, and ecocolonialism of human animals.

from the actual textures of planetary, earthly life but with catastrophic effects upon that life. On one hand: "God", the word that evokes assumptions of omnipotent control; "God", the assumed distant creator and providential controller of all that is; "God" imaged in masculine — even "straight" — terms; "God," who remains unaffected by earthly life and the chaotic fecundities of creation. On the other hand, far apart from "God": "Nature," the wild that is distantly "out there somewhere"; "Nature," like God, is set apart from human living, yet set apart to be tamed and conquered by human "Culture"; "Nature," the eternal laws that shape creation, properly ordered and *straight*. What is human "Nature," we might ask? And the answer that seized control for the past centuries is that of a straight, white, European male — imago Dei in its most anthropocentric guises (Erickson 2015).

What we're wrestling with, then, is static notions of "Nature" and "God." And yet those notions are entwined, pale reflections of each other, ordering and sanctioning the devastation of life in the Anthropocene — we might call it the "Androcene," we might call it the "Heterocene." Put another way, I may be critiquing precisely what Laurel C. Schneider calls the "logic of the One" or talking about Marcella Althaus-Reid's "indecent theology" in a consciously ecological key (Schneider 2007; Althaus-Reid 2002).

My irreverence, then, glances back and subtly rolls its eyes at this construction of "God" and this vision of "Nature" together. It offers a perverse seduction in asking new questions: How can one speak *passionately* of the divine after "God"? How to speak of the complex desires of our planetary life after "Nature"? How can we theologically reflect on the actual ecologies and loves of this planet? Can we love the soil with more wild abandon? What kind of earthy language do we seduce?

Such a love would be a queer proposition, but perhaps this irreverence is done with a kind of divine passion — a passion precisely for the scandalous love that cannot, in fact, be revered appropriately. Reverence would be business as usual. Reverence would miss the longing of our own flesh and the longing flesh of divinity. To revere, we might say, is to capture, to be able to identify the object of our reverence, to be able to identify the strange relationships, genders, creatures, and divinity that make the planet what it is. To enforce reverence in our present day and age is to enforce a respect for tradition, a respect for "the way things are," a respect for nature "out there" which we are most certainly not part of but might appreciate. To revere is to not question what has gone before; "God" and "Nature" are sacred — don't mess with them. Sadly, reverence has lost all etymological sense of "awe" (Rubenstein 2010). In that sense, I might say that my theological reflection attempts to reopen or stir afresh the clogged senses of queer wonder in the world. Again, my fragile hunch is that sexuality, ecology, and divinity are all intimately implicated in each other, every other, and that a queer ecotheology should put that threesome in awkward and strange positions, some of them potentially unorthodox. What follows theologically is thought experiment — a conceptual possibility — that attempts just that. To do so, we turn to one of the most important contemporary figures in queer ecology and feminist philosophy of science.

"Nature": Karen Barad's Posthumanist Performativity

In her 2007 book, *Meeting the Universe Halfway: Quantum Physics and the Entanglement of Matter and Meaning*, Karen Barad sets out to deploy a theory of what she calls "agential realism," an "epistemological-ontological-ethical framework that provides an understanding of the role of human *and* nonhuman, material *and* discursive, and natural *and* cultural factors in scientific and other social material practices" (Barad 2007, 26). She charts a middle way through multiple binary tensions of construing the world through a creative exploration of the quantum philosophy-physics of Niels Bohr. From Bohr, Barad argues a number of salient ontological points.

Primarily, she argues that, "individually determinate entities do not exist, measurements do not entail an interaction between separate entities; rather, determinate entities emerge from their *intra-action*" (Barad 2007, 128). Said in another way, creatures are not isolated entities — "Nature" somewhere "out there" — but *phenomena* of intra-active agencies. Relations always precede entities; difference and distinction are rooted in the intra-activity of previous, multiple relations. And because entities, creatures, emerge and become from multiply occurring intra-activities, their being is always indeterminate, at the end of the day, becoming, and open to change. Matter, creatures, and the like are *dynamic, agentic,* and open to possibility.

Barad is attempting to disrupt what she views as a misguided turn and reductive impulse in recent constructivist philosophy. "Language has been granted too much power," she laments. "Why are language and culture granted their own agency and historicity, while matter is figured passive and immutable or at best inherits a potential for change derivatively from language and culture?" (Barad 2007, 131). Barad is not alone in this effort. A number of other voices like Vicky Kirby, Stacy Alaimo, and Jane Bennett echo Barad's concerns (often directly referencing her) that thought about matter really doesn't take the agencies and creative processes of materiality seriously (Alaimo 2010; Kirby 2011; Bennett 2010).

But it's the particular conceptual creativity of Barad that fires my imagination here. Indeed, she finds a strong, fundamental resonance between an indeterminate material agency with queer performativity — queer performativity as elucidated by a number of scholars of drag and in the oft-cited work of Judith Butler. Most of us have heard some iteration of Butler's argument or another, where gender is not an inherent trait or ontological fixity but rather an indeterminate process, a doing, a kind of deep praxis citing, interpolating histories and assumptions about gender and in their very citation opening the possibility for subverting those very gender assumptions.

Barad insightfully finds both material promise and critique in this concept. She argues that, "Performativity, properly construed, is not an invitation to turn everything (including material bodies) into words; on the contrary, performativity is precisely a contestation of the excessive power granted to language to determine what is real" (Barad 2007, 133). Here, Barad turns to Judith Butler's book *Bodies that Matter,* where Butler struggles to theorize the slippery matter of the body (Butler 1993). Barad argues that here, "Butler's reconceptualization of matter as a process of materialization brings to the fore the importance of recognizing matter in its historicity and directly challenges representationalism's construal of matter as a passive and blank slate" (Barad 2007, 150). Again, performativity assumes a 'process of *materialization*', where matter is involved in the becoming of bodies all the way down as a 'congealing of agencies'.

Still, Barad argues that Butler misses a fundamental point: "while [Butler] correctly calls for the recognition of matter's historicity, ironically, she seems to assume that it is ultimately derived (yet again) from the agency of language or culture. She fails to recognize matter's dynamism" (Barad 2007, 64). Butler (at least in her early work, I might add) seems to too thinly theorize a crucial dimension to the materialization of bodies, those complex agencies of matter itself. Barad continues that, "it would seem that any robust theory of the materialization of bodies would necessarily take account of *how the body's materiality* (including, for example, its anatomy and physiology) *and other material forces as well* (including nonhuman ones) *actively matter to the process of materialization*" (Barad 2007, 65). Not only do bodies offer resistance to representation (as Butler along with Foucault admits), but "natural" matter contributes in rich ways and participates in the constitution of cultural formation and practice. Climate change and global warming are perfect examples of this phenomena, where human cultural-material practices and unruly matter intra-act together in the tragic devastation of our current sense of the planet.

In turning to "matters of practices, doings, and actions," Barad argues that performativity composes a nature-cultural perspective on material production. She argues this active sense of matter as a "*posthumanist performative* approach to understanding techno-scientific and other nature-cultural practices that specifically acknowledge and take account of matter's dynamism" (Barad 2007, 135). Matter is, in Barad's words, "an active participant in the world's becoming, in its ongoing intra-activity" (Barad 2007, 136).

In a 2011/2012 article, "Nature's Queer Performativity," Barad reiterates the queer dimensions of her argument in *Meeting the Universe Halfway*. She notes the importance of the concept of performativity for queer theory and then criticizes typical uses of the concept for remaining rooted in an anthropocentric vision of the world, noting that "human exceptionalism are odd scaffoldings on which to build a theory that is specifically intended to account for matters of abjection and the differential construction of the human, especially when gradations of humanness, including inhumanness, are often constituted in relation to nonhumans" (Barad 2012, 30). A reader might hear resonances in Barad's writing here with Spencer's earlier observation of the contradictory logic of queers as both "unnatural" and "animalistic" in passion.

Barad highlights the strange phenomenal relations and entanglements of what she delightfully calls "queer critters" — of lightning strikes, receptor cells in stingrays, phiesteria (a dinoflagellate responsible for the mass killings of marine life — think, red tide), and atoms — all of which are ontologically indeterminate in behavior and occurrence. The queer reality of nature, here again, is that creaturely performances are different from one occurrence to the next. One burst of lightning strikes completely differently than another in the communication of the atmosphere and the ground. Lightning performs differently as the material conditions of atmosphere differently become in time and space and as others (in our case, humans) intra-actively observe these phenomena.

Queer critters are particular phenomena, bursting relations that congeal differently, but in that very congealing create a difference to be respected. Barad notes the "'posthumanist' point is not to blur the boundaries between human and nonhuman, not to cross out all distinctions and differences, and not to simply invert humanism, but rather to understand the materializing effects of particular ways of drawing boundaries between 'humans' and 'nonhumans'" (Barad 2012, 31). For those of you familiar, Barad is deeply sympathetic here to Jacques Derrida's concern in *The Animal That Therefore I Am* that we not wipe out all the differences between creatures, between humans and animals, but *multiply* them.[6]

Matter's indeterminate performance, Barad notes, is something worldly kin to deconstruction. The histories and memories of these multiple critters multiply just as the world turns. And they trace lines, leave traces, in the multiply repeating iterative intra-activity of world. Memory in the movement of posthumanist performativity, Barad writes, is the "*pattern of sedimented enfoldings of iterative intra-activity.*" "The world," she continues, "is its memory (enfolded materialization)" (Barad 2012, 44). We might say that this "world of becoming," to borrow a phrase from political theorist William Connolly, holds a deep geo-philosophical memory that holds subtle traces of the world's performative shenanigans (Connolly 2010).

"God": Martin Luther's Masks of the Divine

And so, we come to the more irreverent theological shenanigans. With a queer cloud of witnesses in Rossellini, Seymour, and Barad in memory propelling us forward, I want to take a queer turn here too and briefly cite the material of the towering figure of my own tradition — Martin Luther. I desire to cite and seduce his incarnational theology of creation away from its own moorings into conversation with Barad's thought to think through the possibility of what I might unimaginatively call ecotheological performativity. Many queer theorists note the kind of theatricality that 'performativity' evokes — for good and ill — and I want to dangerously risk eliding a concept of posthumanist performativity with one theatrical metaphor of per-

---

6   As Derrida writes, "Everything I'll say will consist, certainly not in effacing the limit, but in multiplying its figures, in complicating, thickening, delinearizing, folding, and dividing the line precisely by making it increase and multiply" (Derrida 2008, 29).

formance beautifully riddled with theological and incarnational implications.

A number of ecotheologians and ethicists have previously turned to Luther's thought to shake out an ecotheological promise from it. In the now classic *Earth Community, Earth Ethics,* Larry Rasmussen points towards an ecological glimmer in Luther and the Lutheran Dietrich Bonhoeffer "that the finite bears the infinite and the transcendent is utterly immanent (*finitum capax infiniti*)" and that, in what Rasmussen calls an "earthbound theology," "God is pegged to the earth. So if you would experience God, you must fall in love with earth" (Rasmussen 1996, 272–73).

These binary languages of transcendence and immanence, finiteness and infinity, are notoriously difficult, of course, but what intrigues me is that this theological commitment leads to, as Rasmussen notes, "Luther's image of the 'masks of God' (*larvae dei*) or God's 'wrapping' (*involucrum*)" (Rasmussen 1996, 279). Creatures, according to Luther, are incarnational masks of the divine, divinity enfolded in the stuff of the earth. These larval masks both reveal divine immanence in the world, Luther notes, and reserve a kind of terrible hiddenness of a divine who, in some traditions, one cannot see face-to-face and live. So creatures function as a mask, a concrete instantiation for the incarnation of divinity where both nearness and alterity function together. It's almost as if, for Luther, the divine is caught up in a kind of queer performativity of the earth, and desires to play, revel in it.

In his most recent book, *Earth-honoring Faith,* Rasmussen reiterates and catalogs some of these moments of ecotheological promise from the span of Martin Luther's writings:

> For [Luther], 'the finite bears the infinite'; nature's creatures are God's 'masks' or, in another image, the 'wrappings' and trappings of God. God's presence fills 'all things, even the tiniest leaf' and 'every little seed.' Not only is the divine wholly present 'in a grain, on a grain, over a grain,' Luther even finds the very 'footprints' of God in those of a mouse. They have

'such pretty feet and delicate hair,' he says (Rasmussen 2012, 198).

Luther's writing and theology becomes a basis for reorienting theological attention to the earth. Divinity is immanently enfolded in the stuff of the earth; divinity curled infinite and infinitesimal in the unruly and strange forces and agencies of creaturely life. Such creation mysticism asks that we reflect on the topsy-turvy material conversations we are in divine creativity. As Rossellini earlier conversed with the imagined and real animals of Noah's ark, Luther's human creatures converse with all creatures in odd ways, and those creatures are indwelt with divinity. "Christians," Luther writes, "hold converse with trees and all else that grows on earth, and the latter, in turn, with them."[7] The finite and the infinite wrap around each other, and the edges blur or transfigure.

Theo-ethicist Cynthia Moe-Lobeda picks up this same trajectory of unexpected divine indwelling in mystical, Christological, and ethical directions. She points to a more elemental passage in Luther where he writes that "All creatures are [...] permeable and present to Christ [...]. Christ fills all things, Christ is around us and in us in all places. He is present in all creatures, and I might find him in stone, in fire, in water" (Moe-Lobeda 2010, 207). Such indwelling, Moe-Lobeda argues, serves to highlight the multiplicity of divine agency, different modes of divine action in the earth — creative, revelatory, teaching, saving, sustaining, and empowering (if elusive in strange) divine relation.[8]

Both Rasmussen and Moe-Lobeda, then, find glimmers of this ecological Luther, unsurprisingly, in Luther's sacramental writings on the incarnation, especially in a 1527 piece called

---

7 For unearthing this quote, I am indebted to Churchill 1999. See also Clough 2009.

8 Moe-Lobeda writes, more specifically, "Earth embodies God, not only as creative and revelatory presence, but also as teaching, saving, sustaining, empowering presence — as agency to serve the widespread good" (Moe-Lobeda 2010, 208).

"That These Words of Christ, 'This is my body,' etc., Still Stand Firm Against the Fanatics" (Of course it would be called that). Here Luther writes the paradoxical masks of God where divinity is "completely and entirely present in every single body, every creature and object everywhere, and on the other hand, must and can be nowhere, beyond and above all creatures and objects" (Luther 1961, 60). While Luther, at the end of the day, still privileges a kind of all powerful, omni-God, we have to acknowledge that this is no straightforward utter transcendence or accessible immanence, but a complex, paradoxical enfolding of the two towards, at least, a kind of carnivalesque panentheism where divinity occurs in a number of guises.

We might call Luther's theological disposition to see creatures as masks of divinity as a hybrid methodological species, a theo-ethico-onto-epistemology, or a theo-ethical disposition *in* creation. Martin Luther's writing itself is performative, carnivalesque, sometimes unethical to contemporary minds.[9] But Víctor Westhelle notes that Luther approaches theological language with a "burlesque attitude," and that, "With his language, Luther brought the carnival to academia, to the pulpit, to the square, breaking down the disciplined frontiers in which these utterances were allowed" (Westhelle 2016, 33). Westhelle surmises that "[the mask trope] touched the people's imagery in which the mask had a very concrete and popular significance [...] the popular burlesque of carnivals, not however in the feast of fools, where it would be routine, but rather in the interdicted space of the pulpit, of academia, and of publications" (Westhelle 2016, 33–34). Luther's writing itself messes with rigid boundaries of specialized academia and the theology of everyday life. It evokes the queer instabilities of those boundaries. And that incarnate instability in the tones of Luther's writing might, in fact, perform a poetics of the flesh, a carnivalesque way divinity relates to the mysterious depths of creation itself (Rivera 2015).

---

9   We might note here everything from his crude humor to his deeply violent caricatures of Judaism.

Those instabilities work themselves into the slippages of a potential ecological vision of planetary life that might both cherish ecological life and take seriously the very real losses planetary life wracks up in natural disasters, predatory relationships, and natural selection. In her "From Cross to Tree of Life: Creation as God's Mask," theologian Wanda Deifelt writes that "If we speak of creation as God's mask, creation both reveals God's presence and conceals it. It contains both the pleasurable and hurtful" (Deifelt 2013, 170). Deifelt riffs on some of Westhelle's work on the *larvae dei* and what those masks mean for creaturely life. The masks that proliferate in the wild, so to speak, "Because God escapes our understanding, we are prevented from domesticating God and limiting the divine to the aspects of creation that please and appease us" (Deifelt 2013, 170). Divinity might occur in unexpected relations, in the wake of ecological devastations just as much as in the beauty of a scene. The wrapping of divinity means that human beings cannot simply "see" divine masks where convenient. She writes, "We cannot just select creation as God's mask because of its beauty, but also because it contains aspects of divine relation we can't fully grasp" (Deifelt 2013, 171). Slippages of creatorliness and creatureliness abound.

For Deifelt however, the inability to domesticate divinity is also deeply ethical. The masks of divinity occur in scorched places, in the faces of endangered creatures, in biodiversity loss, in the ravages of the Anthropocene. Theologically reflecting the masks of divinity entails reflection on the pathos, passion, compassion, and pain that go along with ecological crises today. "To say that creation is God's mask and that creation is in pain (Romans 8) is to say that also God is in pain" (Deifelt 2013, 174). Acknowledging that pain simultaneously lures theology into compassionate understanding, ethical responsibility, breathing with other masks in their labored breaths, and even celebration of creaturely love.

Larval Divinity, Carnivalesque Panentheism

German Luther scholar Hans-Martin Barth writes that, in Luther's theology, "Believers assert that all creatures are masks and costumes God chooses to cooperate with God, even though God 'can and does do everything without their cooperation.'" Barth then exclaims, "God conceals Godself, dresses, wears costumes!" (Barth 2013, 108). This Barth is very excited at this divine fashion show. And I think we can seduce this costuming God, this dress into a kind of cosmic drag show, where divinity intra-acts, performs with the deep materiality of the becoming of the world. *Creation is Divinity in drag.* Divinity lures a passion for carnival, for creaturely burlesque.

I think this metaphorical life of earthy, creaturely masks, *larvae dei,* offers the possibility for thinking divinity and creation in the key of posthumanist performativity. Incarnation occurs in the midst of complex material agencies, luring them on in mutual process of transformation. I might say here that instead of enacting any straight forward account of incarnation — a one-to-one correlation of a determinate divinity intimately becoming determinate flesh — I'm advocating something more like a nature-cultural "intra-carnation," where the divine and creatures enflesh together, are wrapped together, open possibilities of becoming differently, are fundamentally indeterminate, and appreciate responsibility to the multiplicity of divine-creaturely masks. Drag shows, carnivals, burlesque only occur in the creative flow and intra-active participation of performer and spectator. And those masks quite often become blurred or change roles.

Barad's intra-activity might then challenge Luther's sense of holding on to God's independent action and unilateral choice in creation. Or Barad's intra-activity may expand the more radical impulses of Luther's burlesque, expand the possibility where Divinity dresses, wears costumes precisely because the world seduces divinity to, transforms divinity in the infinitesimal becomings of the world. As a number of ecological thinkers have rightly pointed out, an omnipotent God who unilaterally shapes the matter of creation simply re-performs an anthropocentric logic of human mastery over passive nature. And perpetuates that logic in lived ecologies.

We might take the contemporary, biological meaning of "larval" and apply it to these divine, incarnational masks. Divine performance in the world is always an unfinished memory, a trace, a gestating, changing possibility of metamorphosis though indeterminate material agencies of the cosmos. Earth is the materialization of *divine* memory and eschatology as well. In a view of ecotheological performativity, divinity becomes a "queer critter" seducing other queer critters' disturbing loves and ever-new queer responsibilities.[10] Relational responsibility for the show proliferates in the planet and leaves traces for good and ill in the memories of planetary flesh.

Divine incarnation of spirit, then, occurs convivially: in, with, and under the messiness of this queer earth — tragedy, rainbows, biodiverse arks and all. It might be that creatures are wrapped up in biodiverse performances of divinity, that divinity is wrapped up in creatures, divinity intra-acting in water, fire, soil, and air. These performances are the ecotheological version of guerilla theater or guerilla gardening; divinity bursts and becomes in the most unexpected, elemental places, stirring up new possibilities for relationality, speaking back in scorched spaces, and seducing creatures in a fleshy display of queer play.

And so perhaps, playfully, we need a new recognition of our intellectual and embodied heritages as well: Theology is irreverent, particularly in its attempts to speak of divinity, a depth of which constantly lures us to rework, refold, and remake our

---

10 Joan Roughgarden concludes that the story of Noah's ark, at the end of the day, might urge us to cherish queer biodiversities. She writes that, "the well-known story of Noah's ark imparts a moral imperative to conserve all biodiversity, both across species and within species" (Roughgarden 2013, 9). I read the story as being a bit more complicated than that statement, ecocritically. The indeterminacy of the place of animal life in the Noah stories is dubious — the Noahic covenant is made with "all flesh" and simultaneously much animal life dies, is sacrificed, or is sanctioned to be sacrificed at human hands. But her point and ethical stance is well-taken.

categories. Theology is irreverent in logics of God that issue from a creation, boundless and unceasing in creativity. Theology is irreverent in the ways our analogies bring the unexpected together. Our language, speaking of God and creation, is carnivalesque, topsy-turvy, performative, animated, vibrant, constantly changing shape and drag. Theology *produces* queer ecologies, precisely in attempts of performed utterance, known and unknown. Even the most stable or ordinary theological constructions contain manifold instabilities. We can never speak fully of this divinity related to us, and we can never fully exhaust the possibilities of our contextual, ecological speaking of the Divine. Theology is irreverent and lures forth responsibilities of wonder and ethical care where we thought they might not bloom.

But we cannot stop at outing theology for its irreverence, its audacity, its "incantation at the edge of uncertainty," or in the transgressions of that uncertainty (Keller 2003, xviii). We cannot stop queerly playing with and subverting the fantasies that fashion our ecological life. That play is not nihilistic or purely chaotic — it wraps us together in masks of divinity and beckons us to take on different responsibilities or create new roles. Rossellini's question surfaces again, "How could it all be heterosexual?" My hope is to make an eco-moral claim out of this questioning as well. For this particular nature-cultural moment, we must be irreverent of old stories and ideas in our constructive creativity. Ideas of pristine nature, untouched wilderness, essential selves, essential genders, and uncomplicated assumptions of desire and sexuality, deaden and violate the messy and embodied realities of creativity, embodied ecology, and enfleshed divinity. For the masks of divinity absurdly frighten, play, enthrall, tease, seduce, and expose love. They ask us to make a playful future together in the strange planet shaped in human power. Creatures respond in a multiplicity of ways. Creation's quite the "showmance," as my theater friends say. But the performance is never complete: divine larvae are always gestating, becoming something different. And, to be frank, that drag show of the divine and the creaturely must go on if we are to live and adapt, mourn, and, dare I say, irreverently celebrate in a new planetary situation.

References

Ahmed, Sara. 2014. *Willful Subjects*. Durham: Duke University Press.

Alaimo, Stacey. 2010. *Bodily Natures: Science, Environment and the Material Self*. Bloomington: Indiana University Press.

Althaus-Reid, Marcella. 2002. *Indecent Theology: Theological Perversions in Sex, Gender and Politics*. New York: Routledge.

Azzarello, Robert. 2012. *Queer Environmentality: Ecology, Evolution, and Sexuality in American Literature*. Burlington: Ashgate.

Barad, Karen. 2007. *Meeting the Universe Halfway: Quantum Physics and the Entanglement of Matter and Meaning*. Durham: Duke University Press.

———. 2012. "Nature's Queer Performativity." *Kvinder, Køn & Forskning* 1–2. 25–53.

Barth, Hans Martin. 2013. *The Theology of Martin Luther: A Critical Assessment*. Minneapolis: Fortress Press.

Bennett, Jane. 2010. *Vibrant Matter: A Political Ecology of Things*. Durham: Duke University Press.

Boer, Roland. 2012. *The Earthy Nature of the Bible: Fleshy Readings of Sex, Masculinity, and Carnality*. New York: Palgrave Macmillan.

Butler, Judith. 1993. *Bodies that Matter: On the Discursive Limits of Sex*. New York: Routledge.

Chen, Mel. 2012. *Animacies: Biopolitics, Racial Mattering, and Queer Affect*. Durham: Duke University Press.

Churchill, Steven L. 1999. "This Lovely Music of Nature: Grounding an Ecological Ethic in Martin Luther's Creation Mysticism." *Currents in Theology and Mission* 26. 183–95.

Clark, Michael J. 1993. *Beyond Our Ghettos: Gay Theology in Ecological Perspective*. Cleveland: Pilgrim Press.

Clough, David. 2009. "The Anxiety of the Human Animal: Martin Luther on Non-human Animals and Human Animality." In *Creaturely Theology: On God, Humans and Other*

Animals. Edited by Celia Deane Drummond and David Clough. London: scm Press.

Connolly, William. 2010. *A World of Becoming. Durham*: Duke University Press.

Deifelt, Wanda. 2013. "From Cross to Tree of Life: Creation as God's Mask." In *Eco-Lutheranism: Lutheran Perspectives on Ecology.* Edited by Karla G. Bohmbach and Shauna K. Hannan. Minneapolis: Lutheran University Press. 169–76.

Derrida, Jacques. 2008. *The Animal That Therefore I Am.* Edited by Marie-Louise Mallet. Translated by David Wills. New York: Fordham University Press.

Erickson, Jacob J. 2015. "The Apophatic Animal: Toward a Negative Zootheological *Imago Dei.*" In *Divinanimality: Animal Theory, Creaturely Theology.* Edited by Stephen Moore. New York: Fordham University Press. 88–99.

Gaard, Greta. 1997. "Toward a Queer Ecofeminism." *Hypatia* 12.1. 114–37

Giffney, Noreen, and Myra J. Hird, eds. 2008. *Queering the Non/Human.* Burlington: Ashgate.

Halberstam, J. Jack. 2011. *The Queer Art of Failure.* Durham: Duke University Press.

Johnson, Alex. 2011. "How to Queer Ecology one Goose at a Time." *Orion Magazine.* https://orionmagazine.org/article/how-to-queer-ecology-once-goose-at-a-time.

Keller, Catherine. 2003. *Face of the Deep: A Theology of Becoming.* New York: Routledge.

———. 2015. *Cloud of the Impossible: Negative Theology and Planetary Entanglement.* New York: Columbia University Press.

Keller, Catherine and Mary Jane Rubenstein, eds. 2017. *Entangled Worlds: Religion, Science and New Materialisms.* New York: Fordham University Press.

Kirby, Vicky. 2011. *Quantum Anthropologies: Life at Large.* Durham: Duke University Press.

Luther, Martin. 1961. "That These Words of Christ, 'This Is My Body,' etc., Still Stand Firm against the Fanatics." In *Word and Sacrament III.* Edited and translated by Robert H. Fischer. Volume 37 of *Luther's Works.* American Edition edited by Jeroslav Pelikan and Helmut T. Hehmann. Philadelphia: Fortress Press. 14–17.

Moe-Lobeda, Cynthia. 2010. "Being the Church as, in, and against White Privilege." In *Transformative Lutheran Theologies: Feminist, Womanist, and Mujerista Perspectives.* Edited by Mary J. Streufert. Minneapolis: Fortress Press. 197–210.

Mortimer-Sandilands, Catriona and Bruce Erickson, eds. 2010. *Queer Ecologies: Sex, Nature, Politics, Desire.* Bloomington: Indiana University Press.

Morton, Timothy. 2010. "Guest Column: Queer Ecology." PMLA 125.2. 273–82.

Rasmussen, Larry. 1996. *Earth Community, Earth Ethics.* Maryknoll: Orbis Books.

———. 2012. *Earth-honoring Faith: Religious Ethics in a New Key.* New York: Oxford University Press.

Rivera, Mayra. 2015. *Poetics of the Flesh.* Durham: Duke University Press.

Rossellini, Isabella. 2009. *Green Porno: A Book and Short Films.* New York: HarperCollins.

Roughgarden, Joan. 2013. *Evolution's Rainbow: Diversity, Gender and Sexuality and in Nature and People, 10th Anniversary Edition.* Berkeley: University of California Press.

Rubenstein, Mary Jane. 2010. *Strange Wonder: The Closure of Metaphysics and the Opening of Awe.* New York: Columbia University Press.

Schneider, Laurel. 2007. *Beyond Monotheism: A Theology of Multiplicity.* New York: Routledge.

Seymour, Nicole. 2012. "Towards an Irreverent Ecocriticism." *The Journal of Ecocriticism: A New Journal of Nature, Society and Literature* 4.2 (July). 56–71

———. 2013. *Strange Natures: Futurity, Empathy, and the Queer Ecological Imagination.* Chicago: University of Illinois Press.

Spencer, Daniel. 1996. *Gay and Gaia: Ethics, Ecology, and the Erotic.* Cleveland: Pilgrim Press.

Stein, Rachel. 2004. *New Perspectives on Environmental Justice: Gender, Sexuality, and Activism*. New Brunswick: Rutgers University Press.

Westhelle, Vitor. 2016. *Transfiguring Luther: The Planetary Promise of Luther's Theology*. Eugene: Wipf & Stock.

CHAPTER 3

Liberating Compassion: A Queerly Theological Anthropology of Enchanting Animals

Jay Emerson Johnson

An Australian shepherd dog named Tyler illuminated several key questions in my work as a Christian theologian, especially with respect to theological anthropology. He did this in both implicit and explicit ways through the affectionate relationship we cultivated over nearly seven years together, which kept raising paradigm-shifting questions about the human in theological systems. Tyler elicited these questions not only about humanity's relationship with God (the traditional description of theological anthropology) but also about our relationship(s) with the wider world of other-than-human animals and the vast network of ecosystems we all share, which in turn ricocheted back to theology proper — to God.

More specifically, Tyler helped me appreciate better how various forms of queer theory — the analysis and critique of sexually gendered categorizations — could and ought to apply perforce to humanity's ongoing classifications of all other animals. My care of Tyler and his careful attention towards me, in other words, brought queer theory's suspicion of binary classification schemes to bear on the ostensibly "natural" (read "divinely ordained") division between humans and animals. The relative ease with which so many, both scholar and lay, simply assume an essential distinction between "human" and "animal" — a difference most often understood in hierarchical terms — mirrors similar assumptions about the sexually gendered categorizations of the modern West that first prompted queer theory's critical and deconstructive posture.[1] That ubiquitous human/animal divide operates at nearly every level of Christian theological discourse in much the same way that the homosexual/heterosexual bifurcation operates at nearly every level of Western cultural discourse, as Eve Kosofsky Sedgwick persuasively argued in her analysis of English literature. For Sedgwick, the modern invention of homosexuality has less to do with the sexual identity of a relatively small portion of the human population (what she calls the "minoritizing view" of sexuality) than with the means to organize (monitor and regulate) the whole of Western culture itself, or the "universalizing view."[2] Similarly, the putative division between humans and *all other animals* may stem from particular strands of Christian theological doctrine (a "minoritizing view," perhaps) but has shaped a much wider range of socio-political assumptions that now carry significant implications for planetary ecosystems (most assuredly a "universalizing view").

It is not trivial or merely sentimental that my relationship with an Australian shepherd dog refined these questions and lent them a peculiar urgency. Tyler and my relationship with him actually belonged directly to my theological work, which I came to see better because of Marcella Althaus-Reid's theological method. She insisted on dismantling the parameters of

---

1   For an overview of the emergence and operations of queer theorizing, including some of its salient vulnerabilities to critique, see Sullivan, 2003.

2   These views constitute an understanding of sexuality, Sedgwick argues, organized around a "radical and irreducible incoherence" in which everyone's sexual desires are shaped by a sexual identity that is shared by only a relative few (Sedgwick 1990: 85–86).

"legitimate" academic discourse that had previously made me wary of anecdotal or otherwise personal reflections in professional theological writing and teaching. Althaus-Reid did this in the course of her own pioneering work in the confluence of feminist, liberation, and queer theological projects. There, she brought the erotically gendered character of economics to bear on the stalled progress for human freedom and thriving that so many liberal Christian communities have sought to champion. Those projects stalled in large measure, in her view, because of the absurd segregation of theology from the theologian, or the detachment of the uniquely embodied (and thus always erotic) theologian from theological reflection and scholarship. This segregation and detachment qualify as absurd not only because of Christianity's originating incarnational claim but also because such detachment perpetuates (and at times consecrates) the gulf between theological ideas and their material effects. Rather than eschewing the personal and intimate in our theological endeavors, Althaus-Reid urged us to locate our work precisely there, where bodily relationships not only generate thought but also especially compel action, and without any contrived appeal to modern Western notions of "objectivity" that would absolve any of us from taking bodily life (of any kind) as locations for encountering Divine Mystery (Althaus-Reid 2003, 8).[3] Emboldened by her exhortation, I return briefly to Tyler.

I spent most of every day with Tyler for nearly seven years after I rescued him from a shelter when he was nine years old (he returned that favor of rescue more than once and in more than one way). I adopted him just two years before my elderly mother moved in with me, and he taught me on more than one occasion what tenderness and compassion look like for those who need care, which quite frequently included me. Two weeks before his sixteenth birthday and with his health deteriorating,

---

3   I suggested ways in which her insights on this might shape the doctrine of God (Johnson 2010a); in this present essay I am attempting much the same thing but with respect to theological anthropology.

I made the difficult decision to have him euthanized; Tyler died while curled up in my lap.

This personal recounting bears on my academic purpose in at least two broad ways. First, my heart broke into a hundred little pieces after Tyler's death. I knew it would be difficult to let him go but I had not fully anticipated the gaping hole he would leave behind. That empty space has prompted more introspection and on a wider range of questions than I had expected, even more so than when my father died in the late 1980s. To be clear, I was close to my father and still miss him a great deal. Why, then, would the death of an other-than-human animal provoke so much emotional, spiritual, and theological soul-searching?

Second, the colloquialism I just used about "soul-searching" surfaces at least one vexation in dealing theologically with other animals: do I have something called a "soul" but Tyler did not? That otherwise pedestrian question rose to new heights in popular culture and on social media platforms after Pope Francis appeared to have affirmed an afterlife for our household pets and also perhaps many others in the other-than-human-animal realm.[4] In shorthand fashion, the reporting on the Pope's remarks rehearsed the long train of inquiry into what Christian theologians have meant for centuries by claiming that God made humanity in God's own image and likeness (the *imago Dei*). What does such a claim now mean when at nearly every turn the latest ethological research strips away yet another attributive feature that has been deployed for so long to distinguish, in categorical fashion, the human animal from the other-than-human animal? On what basis or foundation can the binary distinction between human and animal still stand in the face of such dwindling empirical support? Do ethological researchers at least tacitly embrace queer theory when they argue that "animals make us human" (Grandin and Johnson 2009)?

---

4   Media coverage of this encounter between the Pope and a child who was grieving a lost pet presented various views of the Pope's comments; see David Gibson, "Sorry, Fido: Pope Francis Did NOT Say Our Pets Are Going to Heaven," *Religion News Service*, December 12, 2014, http://www.religionnews.com/2014/12/12/sorry-fido-pope-francis-not-say-pets-going-heaven.

After Tyler died, the questions posed by his life and death took on added texture when I was invited to reflect theologically on a sexual subculture with which I had no personal experience: the master/pup relationship. Broadly speaking, this relational pattern belongs among the variety of fetishes that populate the broader world of leather sexuality.[5] In its most basic form, this relationship involves a human master and a human pup, the latter taking on the bodily comportment, postures, gestures, and relational affectations of an actual canine puppy, including the accoutrements one might expect to find when living with a dog, such as leashes, harnesses, and crates (and sometimes leather ears and tails for additional authenticity). This relationship, however, is usually not sexual in the more common genital connotations of that word, though the relationship is certainly physically affectionate, much like the relationship between a human and an actual canine.

Note the qualifier I used twice in the preceding paragraph — "actual" — which is more problematic than it might first appear. An "actual canine" as opposed to what? Do we resort to biology and genetics to answer that question? Appearance? Behavior? Who decides which of these standard criteria apply for definitive classification and who will monitor and regulate those distinctions? Questions like these concerning categorical classification have most often been asked by queer theorists in relation to gender, sexuality, and at times race and ethnicity, but only more recently with respect to the supposed and assumed understanding of "animal" as that which is other-than-human. The limits of language rise up here in formidable pauses, not only in relation to God-talk (as nearly ever mystic in almost every religious tradition would insist), but also in animal-talk. Queer theorists wish to make that very point: categorical classification schemes usually (if not always) fail to capture reality as it is most often encountered and experienced. More severely, those schemes are deployed to regulate and restrict what can

---

5   For an overview of this kind of sexual expression, including its potential insights for theological reflection and spirituality, see Peterson 2012.

be encountered and which experiences qualify as "authentic" or "legitimate." Consider just the modest scrambling of ordinary language usage in the following description of the master/pup relationship taken from one of many online communities devoted to it:

> A man being a pup wants to let go of inhibitions, to take a break from the stress of his human world for a time. Human puppies like to simplify their desires and motivations as they embrace a new expression of themselves, one that is more animal and certainly less socialized-human. As a puppy he can wag his tail, and lick his owner's hand and show his feelings in new and direct ways without fear of judgment.[6]

That same online community enumerates these qualities of a pup: bravery, rational calm, openness, virtue, curiosity, and perseverance. To pose the question again: Are these the qualities of the human or the pup? What, exactly, is the difference? And what kind of difference would that difference make and for whom?

A 2005 documentary film billed as a "pupumentary" on the human/canine relationship — more precisely, the human-*as*-canine relationship with a human master — offered explicitly theological points of contact for the kind of inquiry I am trying to pursue in this essay. Master Skip and Pup Tim starred in the film, the latter having earned a master of divinity degree (as one of my students) and was ordained as a minister in the Universal Fellowship of Metropolitan Churches. The film's promotional materials reflect that theological education quite clearly:

> *PUP* follows two gay, Christian leathermen — Master Skip and Pup Tim — as they prepare to compete in The Second International Puppy Contest (IPC), a leather title contest for

---

6   "What is Human Pup Play?" *Sirius Pup,* http://www.siriuspup.net/what-is-human-pup-play/. See also Slave Pug, "Room with a Pug View," *Slave Pug's Website,* http://www.leatherpug.com/pupRView1.html.

human canines and their handlers. The documentary is the first to introduce puppy play — a fetish in which a human expresses the attributes of a canine, most often in relation to another human taking the position of pup handler, owner, trainer, etc. Warm, affectionate, and funny, the film reveals a rarely seen world. We follow Master Skip and Pup Tim through the IPC veterinary exam, where Tim is examined by the panel of judges in a private room, and then through the public portion of the contest, where the two perform before the judges and a large audience [...]."The seeking of transcendence is one of the highest human efforts — some do it in a church, some in a kennel, and a few in both." In *PUP,* we meet two men who seek it in both, and for whom fetish is not something separate from the spiritual fabric of their lives, but rather, is comfortably woven in.[7]

Borrowing that image of a fabric, I want to offer just three threads of what will need to be many more in a project of weaving together critical analysis and constructive proposals for devoting sustained and deliberate attention to other-than-human animals in Christian theology. A portion of that fabric, as I want to propose in this essay, will portray how we might liberate compassion from anthropocentric categorization with the hope of inspiring a deep praxis of care toward Earth and its many animals, human or otherwise. In shorthand fashion, the three "threads" I have in mind are these: (1) rejecting the *imago Dei* as an essentialized category or reified essence in theological anthropology; (2) cultivating practices for re-enchanting the world; and (3) attending to ecosystems of gay affection.

Theological Anthropology and the Imago Dei

I am persuaded that this first thread determines not only the tone and character of Christian approaches to human sexual-

---

7   The online source for this film has since been removed: http://www.wise-orchid.com/pupumentary/film.htm (accessed: 1 November 2013).

ity but also the agenda of Christian theological projects over-all. What or who is the human in relation to God? This is the foundational question of theological anthropology, which queer theory renders more complex, not least by interrogating the no-tion of a "foundation" in any such inquiry (Turner 2000, 1–35). The anthropological query has to some degree always informed ethical deliberations in Christian history but its contemporary significance appeared quite notably in the controversy over the election of Gene Robinson — an openly gay and partnered Episcopal priest — as Bishop of New Hampshire in 2003. The religious critique surrounding that election and its aftermath lacked nearly any references to the biblical story of Sodom's de-struction in Genesis 19 (a text that theological critics of lesbian and gay relationships most commonly cited for decades) and focused instead on more robust arguments from Genesis 1 and 2 concerning the gender "complementarity" of human beings (Johnson 2010b). In short, sexual *behavior* matters only insofar as it reflects that which makes human beings human in relation to the God who creates us — a key benchmark in theological an-thropology.

Whether anything of genuine significance separates humans from other animals constitutes yet another vital question for theological anthropology, which the controversies over human sexuality in Christian churches have posed in some particular ways. When pursuing, for example, what qualifies as a "natural" sexual act, turning to the behavior of other-than-human ani-mals proves less reliable than one might at first suppose (Alaimo 2010). What does it mean theologically when humans appear more "animalistic" and animals more "cultured" than standard systems of classification would seem to permit? Does anything of moral or theological significance distinguish humans from other animals and, concomitantly, what does this imply con-cerning how we relate to the many other animals with whom we share this planet? The first half of that question has received considerable attention in the history of theological ideas (espe-cially with reference to the *imago Dei*) and the second, relatively little.

As responses to questions concerning human distinctiveness have been shifting in recent years, and at times rather dramatically, how we conceive of the status of the other-than-human animal prompts is, in my view, both a theological and ethical crisis. A *theological* crisis insofar as the inclusion of other-than-human animals in constructive theological work would compel revisiting, rethinking, and reconstructing nearly every Christian doctrinal topic (Segerdahl 2011). David Clough makes a convincing argument for this sweeping reconsideration of Christian doctrine by noting that the logic of Christian theology itself turns not on dividing humans from other animals but rather on the distinction between Creator and created. Clough believes that this otherwise subtle shift significantly broadens the incarnational claim in the biblical Gospel according to John: the word of God became flesh (John 1:14) — not human, but *flesh,* a broader claim about the Creator becoming creature. This affirmation of the creaturely God as Creator, Clough argues, "means the subversion of all human attempts to create hierarchy among creatures" (Clough 2012, 27).

As Clough strongly implies, these theological reassessments then fuel an ethical crisis insofar as human exceptionalism can no longer fund religious justifications for treating other-than-human animals in any way we please as long as such treatment eventually accrues to humanity's benefit. More pointedly, it becomes more difficult for human domination to occlude the practices of factory farming as a form of torture, which has in turn served to blunt and mitigate the suffering of disposable humans. Sustained theological attention to other-than-human animals, in other words, makes more visible the extent to which literary tropes and social practices drawn from the world of non-human animals both permits and perpetuates the denigration, oppression, and abuse of human beings.[8] This insight ap-

---

8 I would much prefer to argue more simply that the pain of other animals inflicted on them by human animals suffices as a moment of crisis. But it does not, in large measure, because this would risk undermining the justification for inflicting pain on other humans. The suffering of human animals and other-than-human animals is thus deeply intertwined in complex ways.

peared at least as early as the 1990s in Carol Adams' work on the connections between sexism and meat production and more recently in Michelle Alexander's analysis of the prison system in the United States as a new version of Jim Crow segregation (Adams 1990; Alexander 2012). Indeed, one could read Alexander's work and consider the mass incarceration of African Americans as an analogue of factory farming.

This sense of theological crisis and its ethical quandaries can surface a rather wide array of concerns. The relationship between the *imago Dei* and "evolutionary theodicy" provides just one illustration. Consider first this curiosity: Abrahamic traditions exhibit little if any consensus on what exactly the image of God in humanity entails. Potential candidates populate a rather long list. Guunlaugur Jonsson's survey of those possibilities in the religious literature, which he restricted to the period between 1882 and 1982, ranges from mental endowment and self-awareness to physical morphology, upright stance, and sexual differentiation (Linzey 2009, 28). In the midst of this diversity one constant remains: No matter in what the *imago Dei* consists, it nonetheless sets humans apart from all other creatures, and usually in a system of hierarchical domination. Empirical evidence for that distinction, however, is dwindling. Biologists and ethologists alike now argue (and some have long since simply assumed) that many if not most mammals share with humans some key components for rational thinking, including problem solving and the use of tools, as well as a previously unimagined affective life replete with experiences of joy, envy, love, grief, companionship, and fear, perhaps even systems of morality.[9] Some theologians still retain the distinctiveness of the *imago Dei* in light of this evidence but modify its import; the distinction comes not with unique privileges but added responsibility (Houston 2012, 149). Or as Clough proposes, human particularity refers to having been "called on by God to image God among

---

9 Among the many studies and explorations, see: Csányi 2000; Masson and McCarthy 1995; Bekoff and Pierce 2009; and, for the results of the first MRI studies of canine brains in conscious dogs: Berns 2013.

the other creatures" (Clough 2012, 76). The *imago Dei* in these approaches is thus best understood as a vocation of care, a vocational proposal that would at least start to echo approaches by queer theorists who emphasize behaviors and practices rather than essences and identities in their socio-political analyses of the human.[10] As Andrew Linzey would likely argue, whether human beings possess some kind of essence called "the image of God" matters far less than whether human beings live in such a way as to "become signs of the order of existence for which all creatures long" (Linzey 2007, 39).

These ruminations provoke a still deeper theological quandary that runs to the root of the Christian doctrine of creation. Slowly but surely erasing the line of uniqueness between humans and other animals calls the goodness of creation itself into question. Simply put, how does one maintain that claim of goodness on a planet that apparently runs on the unrelenting pain and suffering of every animal (see, e.g., Webb 1998, 115–23, 174–80)? Christopher Southgate has posed this very question, a form of what he calls "evolutionary theodicy" to reflect the intensification of this ancient problem in the wake of Darwin's theory of how species evolve. The problem stated succinctly from a Darwinian perspective is just this: later forms of life emerge only from the pain and suffering of their predecessors. As early as 1888, Anglican theologian J.R. Illingworth took seriously the theological challenge this Darwinian insight posed: "The universality of pain throughout the range of the animal world, reaching back into the distant ages of geology, and involved in the very structure of the animal organism, is without doubt among the most serious problems which the Theist has to face" (Southgate 2008, 1).

Evolutionary biology did not, of course, introduce pain and suffering as a theological problem for the modern world. But Darwin's theories did extend the reach of that ancient problem

---

10 Nikki Sullivan notes the tendency among queer theorists to resist precise definitions ("new labels for old boxes") and to stress instead a "set of practices" deployed to resist the regimes of the normal (Sullivan 2003, 43).

beyond the realm of the human alone and, therefore, weakened the most common strategies theologians had deployed to address it. In broad strokes, the traditional approaches to the problem of human suffering turned either to a theological gloss drawn from the doctrine of original sin (humans merely reap what they sow as sinful creatures) or to a related reliance on eschatology (heavenly life compensates for earthly loss). But the suffering of other-than-human animals exposes added conundrums and vexations to any claim for the unqualified goodness of creation. Apart from robust notions of sin or some form of eschatological compensation, how can systems of Christian theology address other-than-human pain and still sustain an affirmation of divine goodness with any confidence?

This question has proved vexing to theologians only within the last few decades, and even then without the kind of widespread urgency it deserves. Just posing such questions interrupts a long-standing supposition that other-than-human animals do not experience pain, do not suffer, do not worry or fall into anxiety, or more generally bear no stamp whatsoever of the *imago Dei*. This supposition has shaped a considerable array of cultural patterns and funded foundational modes of human self-understanding that many find difficult if not impossible to relinquish. Experimentation on live animals, for example, whether for purposes ranging from testing cosmetics to military physicians practicing surgical skills, is still broadly legal in most countries. Some restrictions on the most egregious of these practices — such as surgical procedures without any anesthesia — have appeared in Europe and the US, but only relatively recently. Justifying these practices, which are usually grouped under the broad banner of "vivisection," seems difficult to imagine unless one supposes that such acts cause no pain, either physical or emotional, or that the pain is negligible for "mere" animals when it is inflicted for the greater good of humans (who, in this form of the supposition, are decidedly not "animals").[11]

---

11   Matthew Scully notes that the appeal to "science" and "scientific research" tends to cover a plethora of abusive and torturous practices with a veneer of

In short, as it becomes increasingly difficult if not impossible to deny or overlook or dismiss the pain and suffering of other-than-human animals, particularly intractable if not intolerable philosophical and ethical problems start coming more vividly to light, many of which have been part and parcel of Christian theological constructions from the beginning.[12] Solutions to these problems will emerge, not from doctrinal reconstructions alone (vital as they are), but from adopting a posture toward the world of God's creation marked by a spiritual practice of "re-enchantment."

A Re-Enchanted World

The way I am referring to this second thread comes from the work of sociologist James William Gibson and the broader ecological frame he constructs for engaging with other-than-human animals (Gibson 2009). In his helpful chronicling of the progress Western society has made over the last fifty years in addressing ecological crises, he notes the importance of political advocacy, legislative initiatives, and regulatory control. Each of these made a contribution in its own way, yet none of them, either alone or in combination, will advance effective responses to the environmental challenge we currently face on a planet-wide scale.

Gibson proposes enchantment, or rather re-enchantment with the world of nature as the missing piece in this ecological puzzle and which, he argues, holds the key to save us from environmental disaster. Gibson cites Max Weber to make his point and to provide the lynchpin image. Weber worried that Protestant Christianity had installed within modern Western culture the notion of God as entirely detached from the wider world

---

professional respect or for the sake of advancing the "greater good" of the human species (Scully 2002, 380).

12 Andrew Linzey agrees and offers a summary of the most frequently cited reasons for why humans have chosen either to ignore animal suffering or deny that animals suffer at all or to suppose that such suffering poses no particular moral, let alone theological problem (Linzey 2009, 40–42).

of nature and concerned only with humans; "nature," in other words, serves only as a stage on which the divine-human drama plays out. Weber then notes, in a flash of prescience, how this static portrayal of God's creation would eventually render the natural world merely a warehouse of resources for sustaining capitalist development. Rather strikingly, Weber credited this dangerous trajectory to the "intellectualization" of Western culture and especially its "disenchantment of the world" (Gibson 2009, 16).

In short, planetary life now depends on whether human beings will understand environmentalism as deeply spiritual work, including an arduous assessment of Western society's perceived detachment from the non-human world of crude cause-and-effect mechanisms. Margaret Barker's work is just one of the more recent additions to a growing theological and spiritual chorus in which she draws from an Eastern Orthodox perspective to make a proposal similar to Gibson's. Noting the array of competing priorities, both cultural and economic, that keep politicians focused only on short-term solutions, Barker urges a return to the biblical vision of humanity's deep rootedness in creation to inspire a more effective Christian response to present ecological dilemmas (Barker 2012, 4).

I would build on the work offered by both Gibson and Barker to suggest that this "quest for a new kinship with nature," that sense of "enchantment" firmly rooted in the world as God's own creation, entails sustained attention to the development of at least three component parts for such a quest: empathy, intimacy, and compassion. This would mean, in broad strokes, that the slow dissolution of the *imago Dei* as humanity's exclusive possession contributes to an awareness of other-than-human pain and suffering, or *empathy*. Even this modest bridge between humans and other animals invites in turn relationships marked by a profound *intimacy* with creatures and ecosystems rather than only by systems of bureaucratic management and control. Intimate relations can then prompt and sustain a posture of *compassion* and its commitment to a praxis of care.

Animating that relational arc does, however, entail a significant shift in humanity's self-perception and a reorientation of
humanity's position and posture in the created order. A similar
shift in *sexual* self-perception — and not without similar expressions of anxiety — was prompted by lesbian and gay relationships and the queer lens they provide for (re)reading the biblical
account of divine creation. The modern emphasis on "gender
complementarity" in Genesis 2, for example, overlooks what
many ancient commentators would have us consider about that
text.

After repeatedly affirming the goodness of what God creates,
the biblical storyteller has God notice the one thing that is not
good — the human creature God just made seems so mourn-
fully alone. The first attempt at a divine solution to this problem
appears both startling and endearing: God presents a host of
animals to the human to see if any of them might make a suit-
able companion (Genesis 2:18–20), and presumably that first
human could have chosen any one of those animals (Greenberg
2004, 50–51). Rather than choosing just one of these creatures,
however, the human gives a name to each one — not a category
or classification, but a *name*. While some queer theorists treat
names and even the act of naming with suspicion, as types of
categorical classification (Sullivan 2003, 46), they need not of
necessity function as regulatory markers. Naming a creature
can be a profoundly intimate act of relational tenderness, as any
parent of a newborn child knows, as well as anyone who names
a nonhuman animal companion. This seems to be the biblical
writer's very point in a story about a solitary human finding intimacy in an enchanting world of other animals (Johnson 2013,
145–49).

Ecosystems of Gay Affection

The third and final thread of this essay returns (eventually)
to Master Skip and Pup Tim, who might inspire ways to begin weaving a liberating practice from these insights of queer
theorists and queerly related theologians. I return to the pup

phenomenon for help in surfacing what so often remains unnoticed in the first two threads, what I would call the energy of the desire for communion, a broad desire to which gay and lesbian people do not bear exclusive witness, to be sure, but who might nonetheless contribute catalytic insights.

I remain convinced of queer theory's usefulness for discerning various ways in which lesbian and gay relationships can contribute to constructive theological work, especially concerning theological anthropology. Queer theorizing offers this assistance with the critical gaze it turns on the categorical classification schemes of the modern West, the schemes that frame answers to anthropological investigations with binary constructions — male or female, black or white, straight or gay — which are then bolstered and maintained with a variety of regulatory regimes, whether political or religious. As that critical gaze likewise illumines who benefits from those classification schemes and how they do, this queerly deconstructive gesture now needs to reach toward that ubiquitous distinction between "human" and "animal" (Giffney and Hird 2008). Just as the critical analysis of the binary gender system among queer theorists carries broader transformational implications in areas ranging from race and ethnicity to economics and class, so also the queering of humanity's privileged position holds potential for mobilizing theological resources in broader and more effective efforts to address the ongoing degradation of planetary ecosystems. Or as David Abram has urged, though without explicitly resorting to queer theory per se, we need to restore a sense of the human as deeply embedded in Earth, not above it or even on it but ensconced within its rhythms and patterns:

The human body is not a closed or static object, but an open, unfinished entity utterly entwined with the soils, waters, and winds that move through it — a wild creature whose life is contingent upon the multiple other lives that surround it, and the shifting flows that surge through it (Abram 2010, 110).

Extrapolating from this kind of queer analysis, the component parts I proposed for a re-enchanted world — empathy, intimacy, and compassion — likewise languish in categorical systems that classify nearly every relationship as either "sexual" or "platonic" (to use that old-fashioned euphemism), and that further divide the former into legitimately "heterosexual" and illicitly "homosexual." Patrick Cheng has described this dynamic by turning to the Christian doctrine of the Trinity and its resistance to the binary division between the interior "self" and the external "other," which he then maps to the contemporary reduction of all relationships as either sexual or not (Cheng 2011, 56). He recalls Elizabeth Stuart's similarly Trinitarian analysis of the role played by friendship in Christian traditions and both its cultural and religious reduction to pair-bonded monogamy. To those projects, I would add the historical and sociological work on marriage done by Stephanie Coontz, who argues that the elevation of romantic love as the primary reason for and content of the institution of marriage marks a startling innovation of the modern West, which has actually destabilized the institution itself (Coontz 2005). Among the consequences of this cultural shift, she notes, has been the slow but steady erosion of deep friendships outside of the marital relationship. Elizabeth Stuart explains why this might matter theologically:

The formation of friendships is part of the larger project of learning to embrace the stranger, but friendship also serves to break the bonds of culturally constructed kinship and the captivity of passion within sexual relationships. Friendship keeps the eschatological dream alive by breaking love out of coupledom, by breaking love out of the confines of sexual orientation, and sometimes by outlasting other forms of love (Stuart 2003, 113).

Stuart clearly has human relationships in mind when she urges us to "embrace the stranger" and break the "bonds of culturally constructed kinship," but these exhortations surely belong on the wider landscape of inter-species relations as well. What those relations entail deserves and sometimes demands a caveat: I do not mean "bestiality," as many anti-LGBT commentators might quickly suppose. The need to make such a caveat explicit speaks volumes about the peculiar dilemmas that emerge in the process of re-enchanting the world of other-than-human animals. Critics of "same-sex" relationships do not place bestiality on that ethical slippery slope toward ruin just randomly or merely for shock value, nor is this alarming caution new to Western discourse. The same anxiety and near panic percolated in the urge, on the one hand, to clarify the economic distinctions of class in nineteenth century Europe by classifying the sexual relations of the lower classes as more closely "bestial" (Lacqueur 1990, 205), and on the other hand, the portrayal of sexual relations in African tribes as similarly "bestial" to bolster the justification for their enslavement (Douglas 2005, 114). More recently, both Ben Carson (a retired pediatric neurosurgeon and former candidate for President of the United States) and televangelist Pat Robertson illustrated the political and religious utility of other-than-human animals to induce disgust. More specifically, by evoking (unspecified) relationships with (unnamed) "animals" they sought to arouse the kind of revulsion toward "same-sex" relationships sufficient to mobilize both political and religious groups to oppose marriage equality.[13]

Here then I return to Master Skip and Pup Tim, who enact what the modern West has had so much difficulty imagining as even possible for most men but especially gay-identified men: physical affection apart from genital sexual relations. Skip and Tim do this, of course, by performing the other-than-human.

---

13 Carson and Robertson evoked bestiality explicitly as the likely result of permitting same-sex marriage. Concerning Robertson, see Trudy Ring, "WATCH: Marriage Equality Will Lead to Man-Animal Love Affairs, Says Pat Robertson," *Advocate,* July 22, 2015, http://www.advocate.com/marriage-equality/2015/07/22/watch-marriage-equality-will-lead-man-animal-love-affairs-says-pat-robe, and concerning Carson, see "G.O.P. Hopes for Unity May Be Upset by Ben Carson," *New York Times,* December 21, 2014, http://www.nytimes.com/2014/12/22/us/politics/gop-hopes-for-unity-may-be-upset-by-ben-carson.html?ref=todayspaper&_r=0.

Do we lament or recoil from this blurring of categories? Or can this rupture of standard classification belong to what might be called an ecosystem of gay affection, and perhaps yield a source of theological insight? David Nimmons mapped some of those forms of affection among gay men in twentieth-century San Francisco, forms that do not always rely on monogamous pair-bonding, or what he refers to as an expansion of permissible intimacies (Nimmons 2002, 7–8). Alan Bray chronicled a much longer and even more compelling history in England, a nearly one-thousand year history of blurring the lines between friendship and marriage (Bray 2003). Pup play in leather communities constitutes yet another iteration of queer affection. Again, recalling one practitioner's description: A puppy can "wag his tail, and lick his owner's hand and show his feelings in new and direct ways without fear of judgment."[14]

Cultivating inter-species relationships of empathy and intimacy just might liberate our human capacity for compassion, unleashing it from the categorical classification schemes that have held such compassion captive to ideologies infused with both violence and torture. Liberating compassion from its categorical prisons could contribute not only to the decrease in animal suffering on this planet but indeed to the saving of Earth's ecosystem vitality. Making that global leap will seem far less daunting when humans recognize how deeply embedded we have always been in a complex world of (re)enchanted animals.

---

14 "What is Human Pup Play?" (http://www.siriuspup.net).

References

Abram, David. 2010. *Becoming Animal: An Earthly Cosmology.* New York: Random House.

Adams, Carol. 1990. *The Sexual Politics of Meat: A Feminist-Vegetarian Critical Theory.* New York: Continuum.

Alaimo, Stacy. 2010. "Eluding Capture: The Science, Culture and pleasure of 'Queer' Animals." In *Queer Ecologies: Sex, Nature, Politics, Desire.* Edited by Catriona Mortimer-Sandilands and Bruce Erickson. Bloomington: Indiana University Press. 51–72

Alexander, Michelle. 2012. *The New Jim Crow: Mass Incarceration in the Age of Colorblindness.* New York: The New Press.

Althaus-Reid, Marcella. 2003. *The Queer God.* New York: Routledge.

Barker, Margaret. 2012. *Creation: A Biblical Vision for the Environment.* London: T&T Clark.

Bekoff, Marc, and Jessica Pierce. 2009. *Wild Justice: The Moral Lives of Animals.* Chicago: University of Chicago Press.

Berns, Gregory. 2013. *How Dogs Love Us: A Neuroscientist and His Adopted Dog Decode the Canine Brain.* New York: Houghton Mifflin Harcourt.

Bray, Alan. 2003. *The Friend.* Chicago: The University of Chicago Press.

Cheng, Patrick. 2011. *Radical Love: An Introduction to Queer Theology.* New York: Seabury Books.

Clough, David. 2012. *On Animals, Volume 1: Systematic Theology.* London: T&T Clark.

Coontz, Stephanie. 2005. *Marriage, a History: How Love conquered Marriage.* New York: Penguin Books.

Csányi, Vilmos. 2000. *If Dogs Could Talk: Exploring the Canine Mind.* Translated by Richard E. Quandt. New York: Farrar, Straus and Giroux.

Douglas, Kelly Brown. 2005. *What's Faith Got to Do With It? Black Bodies/Christian Souls.* Maryknoll: Orbis Books.

Gibson, James William. 2009. *A Reenchanted World: The Quest for a New Kinship with Nature.* New York: Henry Holt and Co.

Giffney, Noreen, and Myra J. Hird, eds. 2008. *Queering the Non/Human.* Hampshire: Ashgate.

Grandin, Temple and Catherine Johnson. 2009. *Animals Make Us Human: Creating the Best Life for Animals.* Houghton: Harcourt Publishing.

Greenberg, Steven. 2004. *Wrestling with God and Men: Homosexuality in the Jewish Tradition.* Madison: University of Wisconsin Press.

Houston, Walter J. 2012. "Sex or Violence? Thinking Again with Genesis about Fall and Original Sin." In *Genesis and Christian Theology.* Edited by Nathan MacDonald, Mark W. Elliott, and Grant Macaskill. Grand Rapids: William B. Eerdmans Publishing Co. 140–45

Johnson Jay. 2010a. "Peculiar: Falling in (Love) with God." In *Dancing Theology in Fetish Boots: Essays in Honor of Marcella Althaus-Reid.* Edited by Lisa Isherwood and Mark D. Jordan. London: SCM Press. 153–65.

―――. 2010b. "Sodomy and Gendered Love: Reading Genesis 19 in the Anglican Communion." In *The Oxford Handbook of the Reception History of the Bible.* Edited by Michael Lieb, Emma Mason, and Jonathan Roberts. Oxford: Oxford University Press. 415–34.

―――. 2013. *Divine Communion: A Eucharistic Theology of Sexual Intimacy.* New York: Seabury Books.

Laqueur, Thomas. 1990. *Making Sex: Body and Gender from the Greeks to Freud.* Cambridge: Harvard University Press.

Linzey, Andrew. 2007. *Creatures of the Same God: Explorations in Animal Theology.* Winchester: The Winchester University Press.

―――. 2009. *Why Animal Suffering Matters: Philosophy, Theology, and Practical Ethics.* Oxford: Oxford University Press.

Masson, Jeffrey Moussaieff, and Susan McCarthy. 1995. *When Elephants Weep: The Emotional Lives of Animals.* New York: Delacorte.

Nimmons, David. 2002. *Soul Beneath the Skin: The Unseen Hearts and Habits of Gay Men.* New York: St. Martin's Press.

Peterson, Thomas V. 2012. "Leathermen: Sexuality and Spirituality." In *Queer Religion, Volume 1: Homosexuality in Modern Religious History.* Edited by Donald L. Boisvert and Jay Emerson Johnson. Santa Barbara: Praeger Press: 191–213.

Scully, Matthew. 2002. *Dominion: The Power of Man, the Suffering of Animals, and the Call to Mercy.* New York: St. Martin's Press.

Sedgwick, Eve Kosofsky. 1990. *Epistemology of the Closet.* Berkeley: University of California Press.

Segerdahl, Par, ed. 2011. *Undisciplined Animals: Invitations to Animal Studies.* Newcastle: Cambridge Scholars Publishing.

Southgate, Christopher. 2008. *The Groaning of Creation: God, Evolution, and the Problem of Evil.* Louisville: Westminster John Knox Press.

Stuart, Elizabeth. 2003. *Gay and Lesbian Theologies: Repetitions with Critical Difference.* Hampshire: Ashgate.

Sullivan, Nikki. 2003. *A Critical Introduction to Queer Theory.* New York: New York University Press.

Turner, William B. 2000. *A Genealogy of Queer Theory.* Philadelphia: Temple University Press.

Webb, Stephen. 1998. *On God and Dogs: A Christian Theology of Compassion for Animals.* New York: Oxford University Press.

CHAPTER 4

Queer Values for a Queer Climate: Developing a Versatile Planetary Ethic

Whitney A. Bauman

Due to globalization and climate change, we are becoming more and more aware of the "queerness" of our planet. The Modern categories by which we fix our realities, simply no longer hold. The Modern ethics and technologies of control have given way to uncertainty and ambiguity about our planetary future. Once seemingly hermetically sealed categories and boundaries between self/other, human/animal, nature/culture, organic/machine and science/religion, have now been uncovered as leaky and porous. How do we respond ethically in this situation to the real and present dangers posed by breaching the limits of our planetary systems without merely forcing our own "longed for futures" and our own values and dreams onto the entire planet? This article argues that we need to open up to and entertain some different values for addressing the twin, wicked problems of globalization and climate change.

Arguing along the lines of Judith Halberstam, *In a Queer Time and Place,* we need an ethics of ambiguity and unknowing rather than progress (Halberstam 2005). Such an ethic does not transform all reality into the human narrative of progress (whether technological or environmental or both), but rather acknowledges the multiplicity of planetary times and values that refuse to be captured by any singular story. We need what Timothy Morton understands as a "queer ecology" or an "ecology without nature" (Morton 2010). Finally queering our sense of linear time and our sense of ecology may in turn lead to a queering of our hopes, dreams, and desires that help us to break out of what Rob Nixon calls "fossil-fueled dreams" (Nixon 2011). In the end, environmental ethics cannot be modeled on efficient causality and instrumental reason alone: this is the very managerial attitude toward all of life that has created our problems in the first place. Rather, environmental ethics would do well to engage with some models that respect the radically queer, assembled and evolving nature of our planetary community

Globalization and Climate Change: Assembling Us All

Willis Jenkins in his recent book argues, in relationship to climate change, that "our brains are not adapted to problems with such abstract causation, inherent uncertainty, and extensive scales of time and space. Neither are our concepts" (Jenkins 2013, 42). His book is an attempt to examine "wicked" problems, which arise from the twin phenomena of globalization and climate change. This article adds more tools to that analytical kit that might be used for thinking about how to address the problems arising from these two phenomena. Therefore, I begin here with operational definitions of these interrelated processes, which, more than anything, mark our identities as members of a planetary community today.

Globalization has multiple contexts and meanings both good and bad (Lorentzen 2011). Here, I use it to refer to the process of the "space-time crunch" that results from the increased speed in transportation, communication, and production. This increase in speed is of course tied to the use, by some, of ancient carbon at the expense of many earth others. As such, it is important to see what is abjected in the production of this space-time crunch.[1] In other words, what gets left out of "progress" or becomes "under-developed" for many human and earth-others in the process of globalization? What allows for this degradation (e.g., Ruether 2004; Shiva 1989)? Though space does not permit me to explore here all of the factors that contribute to the "space-time" crunch, three crucial factors I want to explore are the narrowing of causality to efficient causality, the narrowing of reason to instrumental reason, and the narrowing of family to the nuclear family.

Aristotle, as is well known, argued that there were four different types of causality: material, efficient, formal, and final (Aristotle 1996, II.3). The material is what it sounds like: what the thing is made of. The efficient cause is an external cause that brings about change in motion or form. The formal cause is roughly equivalent to structural forces and shapes that cause change. And, the final cause or telos is the ultimate purpose toward which something moves or changes. It seems that for Aristotle, among many others, causes were not limited to immediacy. This means that agency, or some form of vitality could be found in each of these causal nexuses: the material itself, some external force, the structure of things, and the ultimate end or purpose toward which something exists/moves. The point here is that, just as contemporary emergent theorists and new materialisms claim, agency is distributed throughout all of life and not located in one place or type of thing (Deacon 2013; Barad 2007).

A distributed understanding of causality and agency is not, however, effective for what later becomes modern Western science. As Carolyn Merchant argued, the rise of modern, Western Science can in many ways be captured by the metaphor "the death of nature" (Merchant 1980). Over the course of a few centuries, nature is turned from something that is in many ways

---

1   Abjection is a term used in theory, especially queer theory, to refer to that which is left out of or left over in identity formation or in the defining of a concept or idea. Here I use it more broadly to refer to bodies (e.g., Butler 1993).

alive, to dead stuff that is to be used toward human ends. Merchant and many others such as Londa Schiebinger have noted that this narrowing of causality to efficient causality also had the effect of making objects out of living things within nature: including plants, other animals, and some people, particularly women and colonized peoples (Schiebinger 1993). In other words, as causality was narrowed to those forces that immediately shape a current situation, so agency was reinforced as power over or control of something. We can think of this narrowing as the historical precursor to the consumer society's desire for immediacy. In a patriarchal society where different races, sexes, and classes of peoples are empowered according to a hierarchy of privilege, it becomes all too easy to mistake one's place of privilege within that hierarchy for one's ability to have causal effect. This is done through a series of "backgrounding" other's agency and focusing in on one's own actions in a given situation (Plumwood 2002). The focus on efficient causality, then, enables a reading of social relations back in to the natural world through naturalizing and internalizing social relations which have been constructed over time, what Foucault identifies as biopower and biopolitics (Foucault 1976).[2] The focus on efficient causality (focused on the result of something caused in the immediate past) was also accompanied by a narrowing of reason to instrumental reason (focus on what might be done in the immediate future).

Just as causality was a much broader category among the Ancient Greeks, so rationality and reason had many different types. Max Weber identifies at least four types of rationality, including: instrumental, value-based, affectual, and conventional (Karlberg 1980). Among the Greeks there were distinctions between practical, theoretical and instrumental forms of

---

2   This type of "naturalization" or "god-trick" is also the concern of Donna Haraway and eventually leads her to develop the concept of "nature-cultures" in order to prevent such naturalization. (Haraway 1991, 189–96). Bruno Latour is also concerned about this process of "freeze-framing" and it leads him to do away with nature and culture altogether and posit in its place "the collective" in an attempt to bring nature back into the political realm (Latour 2004).

rationality. Practical asks the more complicated ethical questions about what one ought to do, theoretical allows for a more abstract working through of various ideas, while instrumental is applied in order to bring about a desired effect. Again, during the modern Western scientific revolution, the reduction of agency to immediacy was mirrored by a reduction of reason to the instrumental variety. The question became, what can we get out of the world or what can the rest of nature do for "us" (however defined), rather than what our place is in the world in relationship to other entities. Again, this type of rationality, what we might call a rationality of immediacy or a self-serving rationality, is enabled by a reading of one's privileged position in a social hierarchy back into the rest of the natural world. Instrumental rationality, in other words, is much easier to execute the higher you are on the political and economic spectrum. From a privileged perspective — perhaps, noble, clerical, wealthy, and/ or male — one can easily background the relationality that is constitutive of a given situation, and ask how that situation can benefit the individual. Furthermore, the more social, political, and economic capital one has, the more he/she is able to act "as if" he/she is an isolated individual and bring his/her desired outcome into reality.

Lest I be charged with making a simplistic argument, I am not arguing that the narrowing of reason to instrumental reason and the narrowing of causality to efficient causality was a total or intentional move. It is not a new argument that modern Western science and the process of colonization go hand in hand (Pratt 1992). As the European colonizers spread across the globe their aim was to bring resources back to the center of the empire. This economic aim benefited from the narrowing of causes to efficient causes, and the narrowing of reason to instrumental reason. It is what enabled the claim of *terra nullius* and thus what enabled the projection of the needs and desires of the colonizers onto lands and resources that were indeed inhabited by many human and earth others. Many positionalities throughout the colonial hierarchy were excluded from this way of producing knowledge and its spoils. These very positionalities — the abject — came back to haunt the narrowing of the world to the confines of modern, western science, a point to which I will return. First, however, I want to outline one final ordering of the world that needed to be in place for the "productionist" model of modern Western science, economics, and politics to be transformed into first the industrial revolution and later globalizing neo-liberal capitalism (Thompson 1995).

As is well known, thanks in large part to the work of queer theorists, the production of the nuclear family is to a large extent a product of the Victorian Era (Foucault 1976). Of course such a nuclear family is dependent upon the construction of heteronormativity, patriarchal gender roles, and childhood, all of which were in place by the Victorian era. How does such a narrowing of the family relate to the narrowing of causality and reason in the productionist model of Modern science? First, the narrowing of family to the nuclear helps to transform "the commons" into private property (owned by individual families) and social welfare concerns into "private" family concerns (Halberstam 2011, 72). What was once a communal or state responsibility becomes more and more the responsibility of the individual family unit (with its so-called "head" of the household assuming control over the supposed "body" of the household). Second, these individual units become more manageable, taxable, and accountable to the productionist model of science (medical, political, economic, and otherwise): without social welfare, each family is responsible for its own housing, daily bread, education, etc. Such a narrowing of "family" helps to shift concern from the polis and public good (a very messy and inefficient entity) toward the immediate concern of what is good for "me and my immediate family". Of course, the abject in this model are the insane, elderly, widowed, orphaned, unmarried, enslaved, disabled, and poor who often face in various ways more difficulties than others in modern Western societies. This model of family has an efficient way of dealing with the responsibility of raising the next generation, inheritance, and units of consumption, one that models the narrowing of causality to efficient and reasoning to instrumental. One is also reminded here of the efficiency of Freudian psychology, which tends to narrow all of one's psychology to the parental figures. Or the ways in which parents (often women) are blamed for the bad behaviors of their children. In any event, this reduction of family has social, economic, political, and legal implications.

With the reduction of causality (agency) to efficient causality (looking to the past), the reduction of reason (thought) to instrumental reason (thinking about the future), and the reduction of the family (social) to the nuclear family (the unit of the present) the world is transformed so as to confirm these reductions. In other words, these three pillars of the truth regime of industrial (and later global) capitalism transform the world according to their specifications: turn the dials to these three settings and you get the type of global capitalism we have today. This becomes the context for the transformation of the planet that we think of now as "global climate change." Ironically it is this very reaction to the human forces of globalization on the part of the planetary community that is now beginning to open us up to a much "queerer" understanding of the planetary community than we had before.

Listening to the Ecological Abject: Lessons from the End of Nature

Bill McKibben's infamous book and statement that global climate change and human actions have ended "nature" as a category of life that is somehow separate from human influence is now widely affirmed by the idea that we are entering the geological era of the Anthropocene (McKibben 1989).[3] Even the most adamant advocates of wilderness would likely not disagree that human forces of climate change have now placed the planet on an uncertain journey and that this changes every place and everything on the planet. I do not want to simply rehash these

---

3   I have critiqued this language of the "anthropocene" for leveling humanity as if all humans are equally responsible, and for denying agency to the rest of the natural world (Bauman 2015).

arguments here, but would, rather, argue that from the perspective of performative identities, these planetary changes have a silver lining. Rather than narrating the end of nature, climate change and globalization are helping us to understand that nature is agential and always in process; rather than just being in the period of the sixth great extinction, we are beginning to understand more deeply our interrelatedness and co-constructedness with the rest of the natural world; and rather than merely responding with scenarios for how to manage climate change, we have an opportunity to do some deep interspecies listening and unknowing and focus on the indeterminacy of the planetary future.

In the old debate among feminists (and others) about whether identity is "essential" or "constructed," Judith Butler's notion of performativity offers a third way. In her book *Bodies That Matter*, she means the word "matter" in a two-fold sense: bodies matter in terms of how one becomes in the world, and they are also mattered by ideas and other bodies in the world. In other words identities, bodies, entities, are constituted and formed through their relations rather than *a priori* or *a posteriori*. She writes, "The power of the terms 'women' or 'democracy' is *not* derived from their ability to describe adequately or comprehensively a political reality that *already* exists; on the contrary, the political signifier becomes politically efficacious by instituting and sustaining a set of connections as political reality" (Butler 1993, 210). This process of co-construction is made clearer through her understanding of performativity.

Performativity does not mean that we just perform an identity that we choose. Rather, it means that we are born into habits of becoming in certain ways, depending upon the time and place in which we are born in to. Depending upon our positionality within these worlds according to our embodiments, there are certain habits or norms for performing "successfully" as male, female, straight, gay, white, human, American, successful, etc. However, there is no single embodiment of the ideal of any of these norms, and no one performs any identity perfectly. This is why Butler claims that we are all always "in drag" to greater or lesser degrees (Butler 1990). It is in the remainder, the abject, in what is left out of our mattering bodies' attempts to live into these ideals, that possibilities for changing the norms and our performances of these norms emerge. Karen Barad, in her book *Meeting the Universe Halfway*, extends this notion of performativity beyond its implications for humans to the rest of the natural world (2007). She suggests that if we take Niels Bohr's understanding of quantum indeterminacy seriously, then at least at the quantum level of reality the universe is not pre-determined but there is some amount of "indecision" as to which way the universe becomes. As a metaphor, this performative nature of life might be extended to all other levels of life: to the cellular, the organism, the ecosystem, the planet, the galaxy and even the universe. If this is the case, then we really do live in a universe that is pregnant with multiple, and even not-yet-known, possibilities.

In such a universe (or rather multiverse?) the future of this planet is not bound to our preconceived notions of it or any other future conceptions of it; rather, it truly is an open, evolving, planetary community. Heidegger's understanding of the violence that takes place when we make the world "standing reserve" toward human ends again becomes relevant here (1977). We ought not force the world to fit into our own conceptions because this inherently reduces the world to human efficient causality and instrumental reason. Such reductionism allows for the speed of fossil fueled realities, but creates much violence in its wake. In this sense, we need models such as found in emergence theory, in Deleuzian assemblages, in hybrid and queer combinations, and even hyper-objects to help think us out of our tendencies toward making the entire world relevant only as it is relevant toward human ends (e.g., Deleuze and Guattari 1987; Morton 2013). These and other queer sensibilities might help us to break out of the thought-habits of modern scientific reduction, and help open us on to our always and already intractability from evolving earth-others. Rather than describe some of these models for ontology, metaphysics, and identity, I spend the rest of this article working out some components of what queering the planet might imply.

Queer Possibilities for a Queer Planet

> Queer subcultures produce alternative temporalities by allowing their participants to believe that their futures can be imagined according to logics that lie outside of those paradigmatic markers of life experience — namely, birth, marriage, reproduction, and death. (Halberstam 2005, 2)

As Judith/Jack Halberstam notes in the epigram to this section, queering time and place might help us to break out of the habits of becoming according to the laws of capitalist reproduction. Such reproduction, such performances, I would argue, rely heavily on the reduction of reason to instrumental reason, causality to efficient causality, and family to the nuclear, as laid out in the previous section of this article. If, then, we are to trouble these three modes of reproduction, which lead to violence toward many earth-bodies, then we have to develop mechanisms for thinking about our relationality in different ways. By way of thinking differently about instrumental reason and its role in the time of progress, here I articulate a queer notion of time that doesn't depend upon progressive narratives. In order to challenge the reduction of causality to efficient causality, here I offer a queer ecology in which agency and causality is distributed among and between multiple planetary actants. And, finally, in order to think outside of our nuclear notions of family and reproduction, I end this article with queering our hopes and dreams for the future of planetary becomings. In the end, these queer attempts will hopefully make us much more versatile and adaptable in the context of a planet that is on the move.

The Queer Time of Reverberation

> *It's very difficult to keep the line between the present and the past.*
> — Little Edie, "Grey Gardens"

One of the hallmarks of colonization and capitalist modes of production is linear time. As Walter Mignolo notes, the light of the Renaissance and the Enlightenment projects a darkness over the Golden Age of Islam and other indigenous traditions with which the European colonizer comes into contact (1995). This model of time has implications for one's relationship to history and culture. For starters, linear time inevitably makes one focused on the future as possibility at the expense of the past. The past is "left behind" as somehow backwards while the future contains the light of progress and reason. For many colonized peoples this means turning away from the authority of religious traditions and ancestors. It can also mean turning toward the Western promise of development, enlightenment, industrialization, and progress. As Mary Louise Pratt points out in *Imperial Eyes*, the interaction of colonizers with "wilderness" and "terra nullius" provides the fodder with which the continuation of progress takes place (1992). Once the Western front is closed, the process of economic and technological globalization continues in the form of expanding markets in the "developing world" and in East and Southeast Asia. To a lesser extent, this linear time is also continued through the final frontier of space and cosmology. It is no small coincidence that a cosmology with a Big Bang beginning moves from some singular, original point outwards in space and time, as if in a singular narrative of development. This "scientific" cosmology is, as Mary Jane Rubenstein has pointed out, very much located in a specific theological and cultural way of understanding scientific data. It mimics the logic of a God that creates all (singular) reality, ex nihilo (Rubenstein 2014).

Queer time helps to disrupt this singular narrative, whether we are talking about the queer time of non-locality in quantum physics, the multiverse of cosmology, or the developmental time of individual humans. Nonlocality suggests that there is some connection between entities outside of our experience of regular, linear time; this goes against the grain of relating entities through efficient causality and instrumental reason. The relativity of time proposed by Einstein's famous equation also means that time is relatively experienced depending upon gravitational forces. This is truly an affront to any linear narrative or single experience of time, which is enforced universally. Not all entities play by the same rules or according to the same understanding of time. Likewise, the notion of the multiverse — whether through infinite oscillations or through the proliferation of all possibilities — trips up any understanding of time that might seek to be all-encompassing (Rubenstein 2014). From the quantum to the cosmological level, there really is no singular tunnel of time into which all things fit on the way to some ideal space of progress; rather time is local, contextual, it reverberates within specific contexts relative to the space-shape-contours of those contexts.

This reverberating time, or what Michelle Wright refers to as "epiphenomenal time" (2015), is also something that queer identities experience in relationship to the heteronormative understanding of identity development. There is no compelling linear movement from childhood to family to career to retirement; these tropes don't make as much sense for non-reproductive types of relationships. This is not to say that some queer individuals do not decide to follow in the footsteps of the habits of heteronormative development, nor that there is anything necessarily wrong with specific heterosexual lifestyles. Rather, it does mean that family can be understood as something beyond the development of the nuclear family; that childhood can be non-existent as it has been in many cultures for much of history, or can be extended well into what would be considered adulthood; and that the markers of what a successful career might be fall well outside of any system based upon the notion of "providing for one's nuclear family." Queer time might be at one moment living with an elderly parent, at another caring for nephews and nieces, at another becoming a harbor for stray queers at various stages in life, and at another living in a gay environmental commune. Queer families, as Halberstam argues, are also much more contextual and don't necessarily last "until death do us part": they are for a time (2011). Finally, queer families and queer time are not beholden to the laws of inheritance in the same ways that nuclear family and linear time are. Though there is a "pink capitalism" (and I am not suggesting that LGBTQ identities have not been subsumed under capitalism in many cases), there is much more room within a non-nuclear understanding of family, and thus for an understanding of time and development that is non-linear, to "leave your mother and father" in order to create a new family and community beyond the boundaries of blood (and even species) kinship.

With these queerings of time, perhaps we can begin to really couch our own lives in terms of the journeys of other lives, the planet, and the universe. As in Confucianism, for instance, the understanding of an individual's life is embedded in concentric expanding circles of concern, so here might we begin to think of our selves in such a context rather than in a linear journey moving from birth to death (Tucker and Berthrong 1998). Such a reverberating time, then, might help us to cultivate an ecology of relationships that stretches across multiple generations and multiple terrains (e.g., Jenkins 2013, 282ff).

Queer Ecology for a Queer Planet

> Queer ecology requires a vocabulary envisioning this liquid life. I propose that life-forms constitute a mesh, a nontotal-izable, open-ended concatenation of interrelations that blur and confound boundaries at practically any level: between species, between the living and the nonliving, between organism and environment. (Morton 2010, 275)

If time is reverberating and non-teleological, then space and the bodies that constitute space might better be thought of as liquid. We can get to this queer reading of ecology from many different perspectives, including from ecology itself (Sandilands and Erickson 2010). In a sense, the ecotonal edges of all ecosystems, which exchange energy and information between ecosystems and allow the ecosystems to evolve and continue living, operate metaphorically in the same way as a Deleuzian assemblage or as Butler's performative identity. Each "collecting" of a given ecosystem is an assemblage of various historical bio-cultural flows of energy and information. At the same time, each collecting (or subjection in Butler's terms) creates abjects that are remainders or leftovers, which become part of a different collecting, *ad infinitum* (cf. Latour 2004). In this brief section, I want to make palatable this verbose paragraph with some more bite-sized examples on which the reader might masticate.

First, we can think of queer ecology through the queerness of evolution. As authors such as Joan Roughgarden have pointed out, nature does not promote any type of sexuality. Rather, heteronormativity is read into nature. In her book, *Evolution's Rainbow,* she catalogues many species that are homosexual, transgendered, hermaphroditic, and asexual. Furthermore, she goes on to argue, as other feminist philosophers of science have, that cooperation is just as important in the process of evolution as (if not more than) competition (Roughgarden 2004). What she and others are basically arguing is that heternormativity has been read into the evolutionary record, just as racism and sexism has, by mostly elite men "doing" science. We can see this as well in the work of Linnaeus when he describes the plant world in terms of the heterosexual family (Schiebinger 1993). Once we begin to see the diversity of sexualities in nature, and also that ecosystems and individual organisms depend upon a very highly developed amount of cooperation and symbiosis, then we can begin to challenge the idea that evolution is some type of narrative of progress toward the survival of the fittest or most evolved. Instead, we can look at the various terrains of evolution and how these terrains fit together. In fact, it may be better in the end to think of nature as a Deleuzian rhizome, which spreads out in many directions, has various offshoots, but has no real beginning or end; it just grows. Our breaking up the world into specific things and into a linear narrative of competition, then, is just one way of organizing the world. I would argue that this way of organizing does little for helping us to recognize our animality and embeddedness with other evolving creatures.

My second point is that we can queer ecology through reflecting on our own animality (Chen 2012). We are deeply intertwined with the bio-historical evolutionary flows of other species and organisms: plant, animal, and mineral. In fact our human forms are better thought of as assemblages of multiple organisms: always taking in other assemblages in order to continue to turn those other assemblages into their own embodiments and always being eaten by other assemblages. Think of the process of photosynthesis, which is the process of our very breath becoming the breath of plants, which then capture the energy of the sun and become the source of food for most life on the planet. Or, we might think of our elemental relationship to all other life on the planet and to the elements forged out of exploding stars in the universe (Macauley 2010). Or, we might take the Human Microbiome project into consideration, which suggests that non-human cells outnumber human cells in our bodies by a factor of 10. Our individual bodies then, might be thought of as many unique manifestations of bio-historical assemblages encountering other assemblages in the world. Our own (and other) manifest assemblages only exist and dwell "for a time," before being taken in completely by other manifest assemblages. From this perspective we live in the thick of things, not on some individualized linear path that moves from birth to death. There are many historical human models for helping to think ourselves back into our animality and embededdness.

Third and finally, then, we can think queer ecology through the historical examples of tricksters, magicians and shamans, and radical faeries. Tricksters, of course, are meant to blur the boundaries between right and wrong, life and death, male and female, humans and animals, and humans and the divine. They do this in order to keep the world from becoming ossified into any given human, located perspective. Much like Latour's collective mentioned above, they help break open the collective, or, in Butlerian terms, they help us to pay attention to the abjects and remainders of any given concept, idea, culture, social norm, etc. In a different way, magicians and shamans also play a role in dealing with the abject: they often see what is left unseen and work to bridge spirit/imagination with the material world in combinations that seem unbelievable to everyday reason. Combining trickster figures, magicians, and shamans with nature loving queers is, finally, the radical faerie community. This organization was founded in 1979 and is made up of chapters all over the world. Some of the radical faeries live in nudist communes, while others live in urban areas. The point of them is to find alternative, often more environmental friendly, ways of living together outside of the model of hetero-capitalist production. Like tricksters and shamans, there are often drugs associated with radical faerie rituals and events. They have also created offshoots such as the Sisters of Perpetual Indulgence, a group of cross-dressing S&M nuns who help promote safe sex and sex-positive messages. The point here is that if we are to develop a queer ecology, we must include different relations between bodies within that ecology, including our own. Queer bodies have often been marked as different, and sometimes as "unnatural," while at the same time being closer to "nature" in the hierarchy of beings (Gaard 1997). This positionality, like that of the shaman and trickster, allows queer bodies more chances to think about different possibilities for becoming, despite all recent efforts to co-opt queerness into the institution of marriage. Here, at the end of this chapter, it would be appropriate to think about what queer hopes and dreams for a planetary future might look like.

Queer Hopes and Queer Dreams

Here at the rough edges of this chapter, I want to suggest that one of the major ways we get locked into efficiency, instrumentality, heteronormativity, and linear understandings of time and progress is that our hopes and dreams have even been captured by the lure of narratives of progress and success that flow from these characteristics. This is why Halberstam, again, argues for the queer art of failure; failing, in a hetero-patriarchal society may be just what we need to think anew about what it is we are doing (2011). Might it be the case that we have been duped by our fossil-fueled and nuclear-fueled realities into imagining and desiring hopes and dreams for the future that are literally out of this world (Nixon 2011)? In other words, if our worlds have been structured into narratives of progress that through efficient causality and instrumental reason, turn all of life into fodder for certain human's progress, then haven't our desires, hopes, and dreams been distorted toward creating this reality? Willis Jenkins in his recent book argues that we need to reform our desires in ways that help "make existing economic assemblages work against impoverishment" and for real wealth (Jenkins 268). Accordingly we ought not deny our desire for more, but channel those desires into using wealth to create a more ecologically viable and just world. In the spirit of such reformation, I want to end here with some reflections on planetary hopes and dreams. What can we hope for in a world of uncertainty, of ambiguous relationality, and of evolving assemblages?

Timothy Morton, in an article on queer ecology, talks about how to care for the strange stranger (2010). In a sense, this is the type of ethics we need in relation to future others; the strange stranger is never the neighbor and will never become the neighbor. The strange stranger is the self as well as other humans, animals, plants, and minerals. Dealing with strange strangers cannot involve the complete and total knowing implied by efficiency and instrumentality, rather, it must involve a bit of unknowing: it must involve adaptability and versatility. We must leave spaces for new possibilities to emerge (Keller 2014). Possibilities that we cannot yet imagine from where we are in the process of our assembling will emerge through the proliferation of ideas, connections, failures, and hopes and dreams we co-create with the rest of the planetary community (past, present, and future). Our ancestors really are here with us in this process, as are future generations of life the exact nature of which we cannot even fathom. We need hopes and dreams that are not "out of this world" but that are of, for, and with this world. We need technologies for the planet, not just for human beings. We need mechanisms that transgress our current boundaries for living even if we are not certain of the goals toward which we are working. As we transgress boundaries, perhaps a better marker of progress will not be economic or material per se, but through how those transgressions ripple out and effect other planetary bodies. Such a mapping will enable us to adapt our ethics to changing needs and to be versatile in the employment of our ethics given the needs that arise in a specific evolving situation. Adaptability and versatility rather than "sticking to your principles" or "maintaining coherence," may perhaps be the grounds for principles we need for new ways of becoming that recognize just how queer this planetary process is.

References

Aristotle. 1996. *Physics.* Translated by Robin Waterfield. New York: Oxford University Press.

Barad, Karen. 2007. *Meeting the Universe Halfway: Quantum Physics and the Entanglement of Matter and Meaning.* Durham: Duke University Press.

Bauman, Whitney. 2015. "Climate Weirding and Queering Nature: Getting Beyond the Anthropocene." *Religions* 6. 742–54.

Butler, Judith. 1990. *Gender Trouble: Feminism and the Subversion of Identity.* New York: Routledge.

———. 1993. *Bodies that Matter.* New York: Routledge.

Chen, Mel. 2012. *Animacies: Biopolitics, Racial Mattering and Queer Affect.* Durham: Duke University Press.

Deacon, Terrence. 2013. *Incomplete Nature: How Mind Emerged from Matter.* New York: W.W. Norton.

Deleuze, Gilles and Felix Guattari. 1987. *A Thousand Plateaus: Capitalism and Schizophrenia.* Translated by Brian Massumi. Minneapolis: University of Minnesota Press.

Foucault, Michel. 1976. *The History of Sexuality, Volume 1: An Introduction.* Translated by Robert Hurley. New York: Pantheon.

Gaard, Greta. 1997. "Toward a Queer Ecofeminism." *Hypatia* 12.1. 114–37.

Halberstam, Judith. 2005. *In a Queer Time and Place: Transgender Bodies: Subcultural Lives.* New York: New York University Press.

———. 2011. *The Queer Art of Failure.* Durham: Duke University Press.

Haraway, Donna. 1991. *Simians, Cyborgs and Women: The Reinvention of Nature.* New York: Routledge.

Heidegger, Martin. 1977. *The Question Concerning Technology and Other Essays.* New York: Harper and Row.

Jenkins, Willis. 2013. *The Future of Ethics: Sustainability, Social Justice and Religious Creativity.* Washington, DC: Georgetown University Press.

Karlberg, Stephen. 1980. "Max Weber's Types of Rationality: Cornerstones for the Analysis of Rationalization Processes in History." *The American Journal of Sociology* 85.5 (March). 1,145–79.

Keller, Catherine. 2014. *Cloud of the Impossible: Negative Theology and Planetary Entanglement*. New York: Columbia University Press.

Latour, Bruno. 2004. *Politics of Nature: How to Bring Sciences into Democracy*. Cambridge: Harvard University Press.

Lorentzen, Lois Ann. 2011. "Globalization." In *Grounding Religion: A Field Guide to the Study of Religion and Ecology*. Edited by Whitney Bauman, Richard Bohannon, and Kevin O'Brien. New York: Routledge. 181–202.

Macauley, David. 2010. *Elemental Philosophy: Earth, Air, Fire, and Water as Environmental Ideas*. Albany: State University of New York Press.

McKibben, Bill. 1989. *The End of Nature*. New York: Random House.

Merchant, Carolyn. 1980. *The Death of Nature: Women, Ecology and the Scientific Revolution*. New York: Harper and Row.

Mignolo, Walter. 1995. *The Darker Side of the Renaissance: Literacy, Territoriality, and Colonization*. Ann Arbor: University of Michigan Press.

Morton, Timothy. 2010. "Queer Ecology." PMLA 125.2. 273–82.

———. 2013. *Hyperobjects: Philosophy and Ecology After the End of the World*. Minneapolis: University of Minnesota Press.

Nixon, Rob. 2011. *Slow Violence and the Environmentalism of the Poor*. Cambridge: Harvard University Press.

Plumwood, Val. 2002. *Environmental Culture: The Ecological Crisis of Reason*. New York: Routledge.

Pratt, Mary Louise. 1992. *Imperial Eyes: Travel Writing and Transculturation*. New York: Routledge.

Roughgarden, Joan. 2004. *Evolution's Rainbow: Diversity, Gender and Sexuality in Nature and People*. Berkeley: University of California Press.

Rubenstein, Mary Jane. 2014. *Worlds Without End: The Many Lives of the Multiverse*. New York: Columbia University Press.

Ruether, Rosemary Radford. 2004. *Integrating Ecofeminism, Globalization and World Religions*. Lanham: Rowman and Littlefield.

Sandilands, Catriona and Bruce Erickson, eds. 2010. *Queer Ecologies: Sex, Nature, Politics, Desire*. Bloomington: Indiana University Press.

Schiebinger, Londa. 1993. *Nature's Body: Gender in the Making of Modern Science*. Boston: Beacon.

Shiva, Vandana. 1989. *Staying Alive: Women, Ecology and Development*. London: Zed Books.

Thompson, Paul B. 1995. *The Spirit of the Soil: Agriculture and Environmental Philosophy*. New York: Routledge.

Tucker, Mary Evelyn and John Berthrong. 1998. *Confucianism and Ecology: The Interrelation of Heaven, Earth, and Humans*. Cambridge: Harvard University Press.

Wright, Michelle. 2015. *Physics of Blackness: Beyond the Middle Passage Epistemology*. Minneapolis: University of Minnesota Press.

CHAPTER 5

Queer Green Sex Toys

Timothy Morton

Queer

It is perfectly possible to defy the law of noncontradiction. Like Humpty Dumpty, we should try to believe at least six impossible things before breakfast. It is cognitively healthy and ontologically accurate. Indeed, to say *You can't think impossible things* is, curiously, to have thought impossible things (Priest 2014)!

Within normative Western logics, contradiction is perceived to be either evil or absurd, or some combination of both. But contradiction is everywhere, and it leaks out the strongest when we try to lock it down the strongest. I take this to be a symptom of reality, which I take to be contradictory. In particular, ecological reality is contradictory, and if we humans want to go about "saving," "preserving" or as I'd prefer to say, curating it, we had better allow some things to contradict themselves or else.

What do I mean? It is simply that ecological beings — a frog, an ecosystem, a symbiotic relationship — are intrinsically fuzzy. It is impossible to tell exactly where they start and stop without getting caught up in frustrating paradoxes. Consider the case of the frog. The frog consists of all kinds of parts that are not frogs — all kinds of organs that other life-forms also possess, and that derive from other life-forms. A frog is evidence of an evolutionary process that developed all kinds of life-forms and organs without having frogs particularly in mind. Yet a frog is a frog, not an octopus or a toaster. But it is strictly impossible to tell exactly when a pre-frog starts to evolve into a frog proper. Indeed, the concept of propriety goes out of the window. There are no frogs, in a sense! And yet there are. They are evidently here, with their bulging eyes and tiny, squishy bodies. But "here" no longer means *constantly present.*

There is no underlying frog essence, no precise frog telos. An Aristotle might say that frogs have this shape and are for this thing: they croak and they are for jumping, or something like that. But teleology is precisely what is unthinkable after Darwin. A swim bladder is not particularly "for" swimming, which is why it can evolve into a lung, which has nothing to do with swimming. Evolution science calls this process *exaptation.*

Frogs are made of things that aren't frogs. Yet they are frogs. In a nutshell this is exactly the logic that Darwin uses in *The Origin of Species.* In one sense there are no species, if we take things like frogs to be constantly presently "there" in some metaphysical way, all frog all the way down. Yet in another sense, frogs are not cats. This has to do with the inner dynamics of genetic mutation. It is strictly impossible to determine in advance what counts as a ("false") monstrosity and what counts as a ("true") variant. Mutations are both true and false at the same time; they are *dialetheic,* double-truthed. If we cleave tightly to the so-called Law of Noncontradiction, expounded in Section Gamma of Aristotle's *Metaphysics* (it remains unproved), there is no such thing as mutation, as it involves contradiction. Quite a few contemporary scientific phenomena require us to relax our grip on this supposed law. But the case of ecological beings is particularly pressing in this regard.

Now consider another kind of ecological being, a collection of other beings that we call by a single name, insofar as it constitutes some kind of ecosystem or environment or biome (or what have you). Consider, for instance, a meadow. There are grasses and tiny flowers. Small rodents such as voles are creeping about. A wading bird moves from a river bank into the water. Insects hum in a tree. Now imagine that one is removing something from the meadow, say a blade of grass. Is there still a meadow? Why yes. You remove another blade of grass. Is there still a meadow? Yes indeed. You continue, thousands and thousands of times. By definition, the same logic applies at each step: the answer to the question *Is there still a meadow?* will always be yes. The trouble is, you have now removed all the grass and most of the rodents. The tree is slowly being taken apart, branch by branch and so on — and yet there is still a meadow, according to your logic. But there isn't a meadow — so you conclude that there are no such things as meadows. Someone might as well build a parking lot right here, given that the meadow doesn't really exist. You can also go in reverse, building up the meadow one blade of grass at a time, from a bare patch of ground. At every step, in this direction, you are able to say that there is no meadow, even up to the point where you have the voles and the insects and the creeping wading bird. I trust this serves to illustrate the problem, which is also an ethical and political problem — a problem that has to ultimately do with metaphysics.

The reason for the logic that forces you to claim that there is still a meadow even when there is now a patch of plain soil, being blown away by the wind, is a certain metaphysics. According to this metaphysics, a thing exists if it is constantly present — this idea is known by Heidegger and Derrida as the *metaphysics of presence.* If we hold that ecological beings such as frogs and meadows must be constantly present, then we will rapidly "see" that they don't exist at all. In that case, we might put our faith in something we do think is constantly present. Maybe frogs are just made of atoms, and atoms are real because they outlast things like frogs. Or maybe we can go in the other, "upwards" direction and argue that frogs are made of (human) perceptions of things we call frogs, or discourse, or Geist, or (human) economic relations, or Will, or Dasein. The first solution is scientistic materialism — scientistic because science as such wisely abstains from wild metaphysical speculation. The second is made up of the "correlationist" or idealist solutions of continental philosophy.

Both scientistic materialism and correlationism and idealism are solutions to something shocking first articulated by Immanuel Kant as he strove to underwrite Hume's brilliant observation that we can't point directly to causes and effects "underneath" phenomena, but instead can only see patterns and correlations in data and infer cause and effect from these patterns. Kant observed that there is a transcendental gap between what a thing is and how it appears, a gap that one cannot locate anywhere in given, perceptual, phenomenal, "ontic" (or what have you) space. There are raindrops, and they are wet, and they fall on my skin just so [...] but when I look for the actual raindrop, all I find are raindrop data. Yet a raindrop is not a gumdrop. This is quite shocking, because it implies that a raindrop both is and is not itself at the same time — it is just how it appears (it's not a gumdrop), yet it is never how it seems (it is not just its data) (Kant 1965, 84–85).

Kant himself shied away from his intuition, preferring the idea that what makes the raindrop real is a transcendental subject capable of mathematizing the raindrop as an extensional lump (Heidegger, 1967). In short, Kant took refuge in an old scholastic, Aristotelian idea that at bottom, things are faceless lumps of extension decorated with accidents. Like Descartes, he thought he had passed beyond theological ontology. He also believed that he had transcended metaphysics altogether; philosophy was now talking about data and reality, not about ontology at all. Yet because of his own shock at his own intuition, the Kantian solution to Kant's discovery is the first in a series of *regressive* reactions to Humean skepticism, which is after all the philosophical basis of all modern science. Such regressive reactions as Hegel's or the scientistic materialism I mentioned above try to contain the explosion of contradiction at the heart of the intuition that things are what they are but never as they seem. They try to contain contradiction by asserting something is more constantly present than the phenomena in question. These phenomena are made real by atoms, or by history, or by spirit, or what have you. And history or Will or atoms are more constantly present than the phenomena, which is why they get to be the arbiter of reality, the "decider" that makes things real. When you consider it this way, the regressive reaction is a gigantic case of passing the buck. We still haven't considered how raindrops or meadows or frogs are real — which intuitively they are. The most basic fact about beings, the fact that they exist, remains a puzzle!

And surely this is rather urgent when it comes to saving things like polar bears. If we can't establish that polar bears exist, why bother saving them? Forget trying to prove that global warming exists. We can't even prove polar bears exist, if we cleave to the metaphysics of presence.

Enter queer theory. The powerful insight of queer theory is that at least one thing — gender — is *performative*. In other words, gender such as *male* or *female* is what it is, yet never exactly as it seems. There are males, but not because something is metaphysically, constantly "there." Maleness is a performance. If we simply extend this insight to life-forms, we discover a remarkable and very satisfying fit between queer theory, ecology, and evolutionary theory. Evolution science is also claiming that some beings are performances; a duck looks and quacks enough like a duck, literally, to be able to pass on her or his genome, and that is the extent, and only the extent, to which she or he is a duck. This logic is identical to Alan Turing's account of artificial intelligence; like gender, artificial intelligence is in the eye of the beholder — it is performative. Indeed, Turing's opening analogy is someone trying to convince me, from behind a closed door, that he is a woman (Turing 1990).

There is a tendency within saying that gender is performative towards correlationism, which as we have shown is saying that an observer or "decider" makes gender (or ducks or artificial intelligence) real. But this is not the central insight. The central insight is that in performance, it is impossible to know which part is true and which part is false. As Jacques Lacan succinctly puts it, "What constitutes pretense is that, in the end, you don't know whether it's pretense or not" (Lacan 1981, 48).

If we are going to visualize the kind of entity that we could call queer, in general its topology would be that of a Möbius strip. It is impossible to tell where the twist in the strip begins. It is, as it were, everywhere. The strip is a constant twisting. Likewise, it is impossible to tell where what a thing is stops and how a thing appears begins. They are intertwined in just the same way as the twist on a Möbius strip is everywhere. The strip doesn't require an observer to perform its twistedness. It is always already a performance of itself, to itself as it were. I experience this when I meditate, to the extent that I experience my mind as this kind of "object." What is called mind is twisting back on itself such that its mode (whatever emotion it is experiencing, we might say) is not relevant to some task at hand but rather is simply how it appears at that moment. It doesn't matter, in other words, whether I am feeling jealous or excited or whatever. That is simply how mind is performing at that point. But what this mind is, apart from these transient states, is a mystery. It is "there," but inaccessible, like someone behind a door in the Turing Test.

This bending of mind onto itself has often been associated, in certain strands of Western philosophy, with narcissism, which has in turn been associated with sexual queerness. But it is, I am arguing, a default state of being a thing at all: a pencil, a thought, an electron, a galaxy.

Green

From the foregoing brief analysis, we can see that queerness, in part, implies what I here call *green*. What is *green*? Very simply it is the necessary interrelatedness of beings and the thinking of that interrelation: the ecological thought.

Deeper even than that though, if such beings exist, they are intrinsically green, with or without relation. This is because they sub-vert (*under-green?*) the anti-ecological world that has been gathering in strength since the Neolithic and now threatens all life-forms with the Sixth Mass Extinction event. For the sake of brevity we shall call it Mesopotamia. Mesopotamia has an inner logic, an implicit set of thoughts about what it means to be a thing, and how to act accordingly. This inner logic, always implicit and so reduced to the mechanical functioning of logistics, churns away at the queerness of beings, necessarily violently, since the logistics insists on straightening out what cannot be straightened.

Growing in strength since the Neolithic, despite the mother goddesses.

From what is *green* distinguished? Green is the thought that begins to undermine our Mesopotamian reality. We are Mesopotamians and most of our "world" religions originated in what is traditionally called the Axial Age, the age of post-Mesopotamian formalization of spiritualities.

What is a Mesopotamian? A Mesopotamian is a vector for a certain virus. The virus is called *agrilogistics*. Agrilogistics is a compelling, logistical approach to agriculture that arose in rough synchrony around the world from about 12,000 years ago. The most successful approach was that practiced in Mesopotamia, the Fertile Crescent, where to stabilize changing conditions due to a changing climate, to reduce anxiety about the next meal — and an ontological anxiety concerning indigenous Trickster beings — some humans began to farm wheat and other crops, according to a program that enacted an implicit logic: a logistics.

There are three axioms of agrilogistics. The first is *Thou shalt not violate the law of noncontradiction.* Since the law of noncontradiction has never been formally proved, ever since it was formulated in Section Gamma of Aristotle's *Metaphysics,* this axiom takes the form of a stern injunction. Strangely the injunction was in place long before Aristotle himself formalized it, because agrilogistics works by excluding (domesticated) lifeforms that aren't part of your agrilogistical project. These lifeforms are now defined as pests if they scuttle about or weeds if they appear to the human eye to be inanimate and static. Such categories are hardly stable and extremely difficult to manage (Barbosa 1998).

It also results in the long history of the *Easy Think Substance.* Agrilogistical ontology, formalized by Aristotle 10,000 years in, thinks that a being consists of a bland lump of whatever, decorated with accidents. It's the Easy Think Substance because it resembles what comes out of an Easy Bake Oven, which one subsequently decorates with sprinkles.

If there are lots of people on a train heading over a cliff, it is ethical to switch the points to divert the train, even if the train runs over a single person stuck on the track onto which the train diverts. Only their number counts, *the fact that they merely exist.* Indeed, existing is better than any quality of existing, according to what we will soon discover determines the third Axiom. It doesn't even matter how many more people than one there are. Even the sheer quantity of existing is treated as a lump of whatever. Counting doesn't count. For a social form whose early invention, writing, was so preoccupied with sheer counting (in surviving Linear B texts for instance), this is ironic. Say there were 300 people on the track, and 301 people in the train. The train should divert and run over the people on the track. More to the point, imagine seven billion people on the train, and a few thousand on the track. This represents the balance (or lack thereof) between the human species and a species about to go extinct because of human action. This isn't even a fully mathematizable world, just a lump, an amazing pudding of stuff.

So this implies Axiom (2): to exist is to be constantly present: the *metaphysics of presence.* The metaphysics of presence is intimately caught in the history of global warming. Here is the field, I can plough it, sow it with this or that, or nothing, farm cattle, yet it remains, constantly the same. The entire system is construed as constantly present, rigidly bounded, separated from nonhuman systems — despite the obvious existence of beings who show up to maintain it (for instance the cats and their helpful culling of rodents chewing at the corn) (Rosen 2013, Everding 2013, Driscoll 2014, Hu 2014).

The agrilogistical engineer must try to ignore the cats as best as he (underline *he*) can and, if that doesn't work, kick them upstairs into deity status. Meanwhile, he asserts instead that he could plant anything in this agrilogistical field and underneath it remains the same field, constantly. A field is a substance underlying its accidents. Agrilogistical space is a war against the accidental. Weeds and pests are a good example of something supposedly accidental — a nasty accident you have to minimize or eliminate. As is said, *a weed is a flower in the wrong place.*

Consider the accident of epidemics, commonly known in ancient Greek culture as miasma. The first hyperobject thinkable, yet not directly visible, to humans. Since you are settled and stable, you can observe these phenomena floating about. You see them as para, as accidental. And you try to get rid of them. For instance, you move to America and start washing your hands to get rid of germs. Then you suffer from an epidemic of polio, from which you were protected by not doing so much washing. This is the subject of Philip Roth's novel *Nemesis*. Here is a good example of a strange loop. Agrilogistics itself actually works against itself, thus defying the law of noncontradiction in spite of itself! At least it is when you think it at an appropriate ecological and geological timescale. Such is the global reach of agrilogistics; antibiotic-resistant bacteria may now be found throughout the biosphere: "in environmental isolates, soil DNA […] secluded caves […] and permafrost," in "arctic snow" and the open ocean (Nesme 2014).

To achieve constant presence, not just in thought but also in social and physical space requires persistent acts of violence, and such an achievement is itself violence (Derrida 2001, 162–66). Why? Because it goes against the grain of (ecological) reality, which consists of porous boundaries and interlinked loops, rather like the open-ended play of marks and signs that underwrites the very scripts that underwrite agrilogistical space, with its neatly ploughed lines of words, many of their first lines pertaining to accounting for cattle — a lazy term for anything a (male) human owns. No, I'm not saying that pre-agrilogistical social forms were more present because they were oral. I'm saying that they weren't. Logocentrism — the idea that full presence is achievable within language — is an agrilogistical myth. This is why its deconstruction, in Heidegger and then in Derrida, is a way to start finding the exit route.

Agrilogistical existing means just being there, in a totally uncomplicated sense. No matter what the appearances might be, essence lives on. Ontologically, agrilogistics is immiseration.

And socially, immiserating conditions were the almost immediate consequence of its inception, yet the virus persisted, like an earworm or a chair, no matter how destructive to the humans who had devised it (Diamond 1987, Parfit 1984, 1986, Agamben 1998). Or indeed private property, based on settled ownership and use of land, a certain kind of house and so on — the nonhuman basis of the contemporary concept of self, no matter how much we want to think ourselves out of that. Agrilogistics led rapidly to patriarchy, the impoverishment of all but a very few, a massive and rigid social hierarchy, and feedback loops of human–nonhuman interaction, such as epidemics.[1] Appearance, phenomena, are of no consequence. What matters is knowing where your next meal is coming from, no matter what the appearances are. The physical embodiment of this thought takes the form of fields that surround the city-state. These fields now underlie all other modes of production from feudalism to capitalism to Soviet economies.

Without paying too much attention to the cats, you have broken things down to pure simplicity, and now you are ready for Axiom (3):

(3) Existing is always better than any quality of existing.

Actually, we need to give it its properly anthropocentric form, because — screw the other life-forms, right?

(3) Human existing is always better than any quality of existing. Axiom (3) generates an Easy Think Ethics to match the Easy Think Substance. A default utilitarianism, hardwired into agrilogistical space. Since existing is better than anything, more existing must be what we Mesopotamians should aim for. Everything else is just accidental. No matter whether I am hungrier, or sicker, or more oppressed, underlying these phenomena, I

---

1   On the patriarchy aspect, insofar as it affects philosophy as such, Luce Irigaray is succinct: woman has been taken "*quoad matrem* […] in the entire philosophic tradition. It is even one of the conditions of its possibility. One of the necessities, also, of its foundation: it is from (re)productive earth-mother-nature that the production of the logos will attempt to take away its power, by pointing to the power of the beginning(s) in the monopoly of the origin" (Irigaray 1985, 102).

and my brethren remain constantly, down the generations. The globalization of agrilogistics, and its consequent global warming, have exposed the flaws in this default utilitarianism, with the consequence that solutions to global warming simply cannot be along the lines of this style of thought (Gardiner 2011, 213–45). The predictable result: humans now consume about forty percent of Earth's productivity (Manning 2004, 2005). Humans account for 32 percent of vertebrate biomass. Domesticated animals count for 65 percent. Which means that less than 3 percent go to vertebrate wildlife (Zalasiewicz 2013).

Jared Diamond has called Fertile Crescent agriculture "the worst mistake in the history of the human race" (Diamond 1987). It's worse than a mistake. Because of its underlying logical structure, agrilogistics now plays out at the temporal scale of global warming. Agrilogistics supplied the conditions for the Agricultural Revolution, which swiftly provided the conditions for the Industrial Revolution. Which is why there is a good reaction to the "modernity once more with feeling" solutions to global warming — bioengineering, geoengineering, and other forms of what I shall call *happy nihilism*. Happy nihilism reduces things to bland substances that can be manipulated at will, without regard to unintended consequences. The right reaction is a scream.

Planning for the next few years means you know where the next meal is coming from, for a long time. Who doesn't want that? And existing is good, right? So let's have more of it. Yes, I have just touched the third rail, the population rail. You are now thinking I might be a Nazi. Or that, given that we have seen population growth and food supply grow tougher, I am simply talking "nonsense" (Ellis 2013). Nonsense or evil. Courting these sorts of reactions is just one of the first ridiculous, impossible things that ecognosis does. So much ridicule, so little time. Indeed, even more ridiculously perhaps, I shall argue that ecognosis must *traverse* Heideggerian–Nazi space, descend below it even, through nihilism, and not despite it.

It was based on increasing happiness: eliminating anxiety about where the next meal is coming from. But within the first quarter of its duration so far, agrilogistics resulted in a drastic reduction in happiness. People starved, which accounts for shocking decreases in average human size in the Fertile Crescent. Within three thousand years, patriarchy emerged. Within three thousand years, what is now called the 1% emerged, or in fact the 0.1%, which in those days was called King. Agrilogistics exerted downward pressure on evolution. Within three thousand years, farmers' leg bones went from ripped hunter-gatherer to semi-sedentary forerunner of the couch potato. Let's not forget deserts. Agrilogistics was already a disaster early on. It was repeated throughout Earth. There is a good Freudian term for this destructive repetition: death drive.

Sex

The analysis of the implications of *queer* and *green* bring us to another term: *sex*. By *sex* this essay surely doesn't mean exclusively heterosexual reproduction and its heteronormative cultural spinoffs. Indeed, that form of reproduction floats, in evolution space, amidst a gigantic ocean of manifold forms of sexuality from cloning to gender switching to homosexuality. No: what is meant by *sex* is the uncontainable *enjoyment* with which *queer green* begins to resonate, once it is thought at a sufficient amplitude.

It is logically incorrect to imagine that things are just extensional lumps decorated with accidents, including temporal things. Things are better described as smeared, shimmering, flickering. It is also politically and ethically disastrous. Since it is logically incorrect and physically impossible, trying to impose this ontology only results in violence. It is better to act as if things are as they were described in the "Queer" section: looplike beings whose appearance never quite coincides with what they are, yet is never other than evidence for what they are. An octopus is not a toaster. But the way in which it is an octopus is strangely twisted. A meadow is not a parking lot. Why act as if it could be reduced to one at any moment?

Psychologically, we are used to calling the twist of appearing and being a special word: *enjoyment*. Enjoyment is never exactly coincident with what I think I want — that is what is sometimes disturbing, sometimes wonderful about it. Enjoyment is never exactly mine, yet it embodies me to perfection — it is how I am wriggling at this precise moment, despite my concept of who I am. Enjoyment implies *movement,* and movement is deeply mysterious yet pervasive. It is everywhere, yet movement is one of the most difficult things to explain, unless you are prepared to violate the law of noncontradiction.

Happily, objects violate this law all the time. In fact, that is just what they do when you observe them as carefully as possible, for instance when you isolate them from other entities by cooling them down towards absolute zero and putting them in a vacuum. When you do this to a tiny mirror, you will observe it emitting infrared light (Savafi-Naeini and Painter 2012). This emission is happening without the mirror being pushed. The mirror is shimmering without mechanical input. If you wanted to reduce the ontology of queer green sex toys to a single sentence it would indeed be this: *Things shimmer without mechanical input.*

Perhaps it is anthropomorphic to say that everything is enjoying, in the precise sense of deviating from itself while maintaining its being, like a circle, a line that deviates from itself in an absolutely smooth and consistent way, or a twisted loop. But at this moment, a little anthropomorphism, if it helps us to think and join with nonhuman beings, might not be such a bad idea. Surely the idea that everything is enjoying is *not anthropocentric,* and of the two, I would prefer anthropomorphism to anthropocentrism any day. In a precise sense, perhaps I can never stop being anthropomorphic, because even when I am trying to do so, there I am, a human being, trying to do so — and perhaps my humanness is encapsulated precisely in my attempt sensitively to attune to things that are not me. My chameleon-like qualities, whether they come from mirror neurons or being born functionally and drastically premature, or from some other source, are precisely what make me appear human. As Keats would argue, poets are chameleons, and perhaps this is because being human is about melting into other things, as in how a shaman tries to become an antelope or a bear.

Thinking of ourselves as sensitive attunement devices is perhaps unfamiliar, given how we have recently been thinking of ourselves as "nihilistic princes of darkness" (Harman 2005, 247). But it follows quite logically from the fact that things are looped. It is impossible to achieve escape velocity from oneself. When one tries — *there you are, doing that.* There is no ultimate policeman to arrest all the other policemen and the other characters in Monty Python's Argument Sketch for violating the rules of sketches, because every policeman who shows up is still operating within the Argument Sketch (Cleese and Chapman 1972). Or to put it in dressier terms, there is no metalanguage that cannot be turned into an object language. For instance, I can be disturbed by self-reference, like Bertrand Russell. And like Alfred Tarski I can invent a concept called metalanguages to police self-referential sentences such as *This sentence is false,* a loop sentence that is both true and false at the same time. The trouble is, a cheeky trickster philosopher can come along and bend the metalanguage into a yoga-like pretzel of self-reference. The metalanguage says "*This sentence is false* is not a sentence." But the trickster philosopher can then say *This is not a sentence,* which is even "worse" and weirder — more tightly twisted — than *This sentence is false,* because now the sentence is denying its very sentence-being, not just what it is saying.

Like bacteria adapting to antibacterial soap — and there is a tight link between such feedback loops and the logical loops I am describing — sentences escape the law of noncontradiction and wriggle around themselves all the time. We experience enjoyment as a disturbing parasite that is joined to me inextricably yet transcends me at the same time. Enjoyment and myself exist in a weird symbiosis, like a lichen or indeed like my bacterial microbiome. An ecological being such as a meadow or a polar bear or the entire biosphere is precisely a paradoxical being that exceeds itself without not-being itself. An ecological being is a constantly twisting deviation that is none other than it appears. This is because *everything is like that.*

A thing is a loop, and another way of saying that is that a thing is penetrating itself such that the tail and head end of a thing become impossible to distinguish, as in the ancient idea of the ouroboros. A thing is having sex with itself, let alone with other beings. It is just that we have tended in Western philosophy and religion — let alone left cultural critique — to denigrate this basic phenomenon as narcissism. But as Jacques Derrida argues, there is not narcissism and non-narcissism, there are only various *narcissisms*:

> There is not narcissism and non-narcissism; there are narcissisms that are more or less comprehensive, generous, open, extended. What is called non-narcissism is in general but the economy of a much more welcoming, hospitable narcissism [...] without a movement of narcissistic reappropriation, the relation to the other would be absolutely destroyed, it would be destroyed in advance. (Derrida 1995, 199)

Likewise in the spirituality systems that reside in the strangely cordoned off VIP lounges of Axial Age religions — agrilogistical religions that is — there is some notion of self-existing, self-looping wisdom such as the Hindu or Buddhist jnana or the Christian gnosis (terms that stem from the same root). As Jeffrey Kripal asserts, gnosis is *thinking having sex with itself*: thought in a loop (Kripal 2006, 125). Thought in a state of deviant enjoyment. The most basic thought, thought in a vacuum close to absolute zero as it were, is a shimmering without mechanical input that could otherwise be described as a looping. And just as sex evolved chronologically before humans and antelopes — and indeed daisies and oak trees — there is something ontologically fundamental about the category of sex. Things are queer and green and sexual.

Toys

What are these queer, green sex beings? They are toys. Toys are contingent. Toys are fragile. Toys are connective. And most significantly, toys are playful. To play is to violate the law of non-contradiction. When my cat nips me, she is saying *This is a bite and this is not a bite* at the same time (Bateson 2000). Apparently my cat is more relaxed than some humans about logical laws that have never been proved. Play is already implied by the paraconsistent logic of allowing some things to violate the law of noncontradiction — a violation that a growing number of logicians are willing to tolerate, and which quantum theorists must tolerate all the time (Priest 2006).

The "sexuality" of a thing, how it shimmers without mechanical input, looped into itself in a pretzel logic that looks to some like narcissism, is an index of its contingency and fragility. Even the most powerful object in the universe, a black hole, that cannot be destroyed by anything else, is fragile in the sense that its deviation from itself eventually eats itself up: it emits enough Hawking radiation and evaporates. Things are impermanent in their very selves, not because they are bland extensional plastic lumps waiting for some bigger, badder lump to blow them away. Coexistence, which is an open word for ecological being, is a state in which entities allow one another to be fragile in just this way. To be toys.

Any system of interrelated beings — an ecosystem for instance — is contingent and fragile too. It is also a toy. This means that no ecological action can be complete or absolutely correct. If I am nice to bunny rabbits, it means I'm not being nice to bunny rabbit parasites. The critical game of spot the hypocrite, which has been the most popular way of performing intelligence in modernity, is now obsolete in an age of growing ecological awareness, because it simply cannot function — there is no cynical position that is not immune from the hypocrisy of being unable to account for absolutely everything, precisely because as we have seen there is no pure, clean metalanguage. It is just as the post-structuralists thought, only more so — not only epistemologically, but ontologically. We cannot totalize because beings are never complete in themselves, whether or not we are thinking them.

Thus an age of ecological ethics and politics cannot impose a top-down, one-size-fits-all, political or economic system. It would be ontologically impossible and thus violent to try to do so. That has been what is wrong with agrilogistics; whether soviet or capitalist or feudal (or any other number of economic systems), agrilogistics implies one system to rule them all, a narrow temporality pipe made of grey concrete that gradually sucks all life-forms into its destructive orbit. Humans need to create as many temporality pipes as possible, as many affiliations of humans and nonhumans as possible. Ecological politics is more like anarchism than any other political modality.

There is no absolute space, no neutral, universal container into which everything can fit. Indeed, it is *this* concept, not the idea of place, that is the anthropocentric one. The Newtonian idea of time and space as an absolute, linear container made of atomic spatiotemporal parts is a good-enough-to-be-getting-along-with, human scale tool useful if you want to plough a field or invade Poland. But if you want to slingshot around a black hole or be nice to bunny rabbits, the idea of space is absolutely useless. It would be better instead to de-anthropocentrize the idea of place. Rather than considering place as some pathetic human-flavored candy decorating a bland extensional world of atomic spatiotemporal components, it would be best to consider place as the weird way in which an object deviates from itself. An object emits place, like an octopus emitting ink, or a star emitting light, or like the way in which I am surrounded and permeated by a bacterial microbiome in such a way that there is actually more bacterial DNA than Timothy Morton DNA — as a structural condition for Timothy Morton existing at all. Ecological awareness is just the creeping realization that everything has or emits place, not just humans. The biosphere is its own place, and we inhabit our place inside it. What is disturbing is that place is no longer a cozy human construct at all, one that we can cherish nostalgically or primitivistically, or laugh at contemptuously for being out of date. Place is just another way of saying that things play.

Thinking ecologically has nothing to do with normative purity or nature discourses in which things never deviate from themselves and in which loops such as desire are evil. Thinking ecologically precisely means thinking that things are queer green sex toys.

References

Agamben, Giorgio. 1998. *Homo Sacer: Sovereign Power and Bare Life*. Stanford: Stanford University Press.

Barbosa, Pedro, ed.. 1998. *Conservation Biological Control*. San Diego: Harcourt Brace.

Cleese, John and Graham Chapman. 1972. "Argument Clinic." *Monty Python's Flying Circus*. BBC.

Bateson, Gregory. 2000. "A Theory of Play and Fantasy." In *Steps to an Ecology of Mind*. Chicago: University of Chicago Press. 177–93.

Derrida, Jacques. 2001. "Violence and Metaphysics." In *Writing and Difference*. Translated by Alan Bass. London: Routledge. 162–66.

———. 1995. "There Is No One Narcissism: Autobiophotographies." In *Points: Interviews 1974–1994*. Edited by Elisabeth Weber. Translated by Peggy Kamuf et al. Stanford: Stanford University Press. 196–215.

Diamond, Jared. 1987. "The Worst Mistake in the History of the Human Race." *Discover Magazine* (May). 64–66.

Driscoll, Carlos A. 2009. "The Taming of the Cat." *Scientific American* 300.6 (June). 68–75.

Ellis, Erle. 2013. "Overpopulation Is Not the Problem." *New York Times,* September 13. http://www.nytimes. com/2013/09/14/opinion/overpopulation-is-not-the-problem.html.

Everding, Gerry. 2013. "Cat Domestication Traced to Chinese Farmers 5,300 Years Ago." *Washington University St. Louis Newsroom*, December 16. https://news.wustl.edu/news/Pages/26273.aspx.

Gardiner, Stephen M. 2011. *A Perfect Moral Storm: The Ethical Tragedy of Climate Change*. New York: Oxford University Press.

Harman, Graham. 2005. *Guerrilla Metaphysics: Phenomenology and the Carpentry of Things*. Chicago: Open Court.

Heidegger, Martin. 1967. *What Is a Thing?* Translated by W.B. Barton and Vera Deutsch. Chicago: Henry Regnery.

Hu, Yaowu et al. 2014. "Earliest Evidence for Commensal Processes of Cat Domestication." PNAS 111.1 (January 7). 116–20.

Irigaray, Luce. 1985. *This Sex Which Is Not One*. Translated by Catherine Porter and Carolyn Burke. Ithaca: Cornell University Press.

Kant, Immanuel. 1965. *Critique of Pure Reason*. Translated by Norman Kemp Smith. Boston and New York: Bedford/St. Martin's.

Kripal, Jeffrey. 2006. *The Serpent's Gift: Gnostic Reflections on the Study of Religion*. Chicago: University of Chicago Press.

Lacan, Jacques. 1981. *Le séminaire, Livre III: Les psychoses*. Paris: Editions de Seuil.

Manning, Richard. 2004. "The Oil We Eat," http://www.wesjones.com/oilweeat.htm.

———. 2005. *Against the Grain: How Agriculture Has Hijacked Civilization*. New York: North Point.

Nesme, Joseph et al. 2014. "Large-Scale Metagenomic-Based Study of Antibiotic Resistance in the Environment." *Current Biology* 24.1–5 (May). http://dx.doi.org/10.1016/j.cub.2014.03.036. 1–3.

Parfit, Derek. 1984. *Reasons and Persons*. New York: Oxford University Press.

———. 1986. "Overpopulation and the Quality of Life." In *Applied Ethics*. Edited by Peter Singer. New York: Oxford University Press. 145–64.

Priest, Graham. 2014. "Beyond True and False." *Aeon*, May 5.

———. 2006. *Contradiction: A Study of the Transconsistent*. Oxford: Oxford University Press.

Rosen, Rebecca J. 2013. "How Humans Invented Cats." *The Atlantic*, December 16. http://www.theatlantic.com/technology/archive/2013/12/how-humans-created-cats/282391.

Safavi-Naeini, Amir H., Jasper Chan, Jeff T. Hill, T. P. Mayer Alegre, Alex Krause, and Oskar Painter. 2012. "Observation of Quantum Motion of a Nanomechanical Resonator," in *Physical Review Letters* 108.3 (January 17). https://doi.org/10.1103/PhysRevLett.108.033602.

Turing, Alan. 1990. "Computing Machinery and Intelligence."
    In Margaret A. Boden, ed., *The Philosophy of Artificial Intel-
    ligence.* Oxford and New York: Oxford University Press.
    40–66.
Zalasiewicz, Jan. 2013. "The Geological Basis for the Anthro-
    pocene." Paper given at "The History of Politics of the
    Anthropocene" conference, University of Chicago, Chicago,
    Illinois, May 17–18.

Contributing Authors

Whitney Bauman is Associate Professor of Religious Studies at Florida International University in Miami. He teaches and lectures on science and religion, religion and nature, and religion and queer theory. His books include *Religion and Ecology: Developing a Planetary Ethic* (Columbia University Press, 2014), *Theology Creation and Environmental Ethics* (Routledge, 2009), with Lucas Johnston *Science and Religion: One Planet, Many Possibilities* (Routledge, 2014), and with Kevin O'Brien and Richard Bohannon, *Grounding Religion: A Field Guide to the Study of Religion and Ecology* (Routledge, 2010). He is currently working on a manuscript that examines the religious influences on Ernst Haeckel's understanding of the natural world.

Jacob J. Erickson is Assistant Professor of Theological Ethics at Trinity College Dublin. His current work, *A Theopoetics of the Earth* attempts to evoke an ecotheology of planetary conviviality—the cherishing of life together—in the midst of current ecological crises, emerging perspectives in the wake of global warming, and new challenges in energy production. Erickson is a contributor to *Living Traditions and Universal Conviviality: Prospects and Challenges for Peace in Multireligious Communities,* eds. Roland Faber and Santiago Slabodsky (Lexington Books, 2016), *For Our Common Home,* eds. John Cobb and Ignacio Castuera (Process Century Press, 2016), *Divine Multiplicity*, eds. Wesley Ariarajah and Christopher Boesel (Fordham Press, 2014) and *Divinanimality: Animal Theory, Creaturely Theology*, ed. Stephen Moore (Fordham Press, 2014).

Jay Johnson is Senior Director of the Pacific School of Religion's Center for Lesbian and Gay Studies in Religion and Ministry and Core Doctoral Faculty Member at the Graduate Theological Union. His research interests include bridging academic theology and movements for social change, and theological anthropology and the place of other-than-human-animals in Christian theology. His books include: *Peculiar Faith: Queer Theology for Christian Witness* (Seabury Books, 2014), *Divine Communion: A Eucharistic Theology of Sexual Intimacy* (Seabury Books, 2013), *Queer Religion* (two volumes, with Donald Boisvert; Praeger, 2011), and *Dancing with God: Anglican Christianity and the Practice of Hope* (Morehouse, 2005).

Timothy Morton is the Rita Shea Guffey Chair in English at Rice University. His works include: *Nothing: Three Inquiries in Buddhism and Critical Theory* (Chicago, 2015), *Hyperobjects: Philosophy and Ecology after the End of the World* (Minnesota, 2013), *Realist Magic: Objects, Ontology, Causality* (Open Humanities, 2013), *The Ecological Thought* (Harvard, 2010), *Ecology without Nature* (Harvard, 2007), seven other books and one hundred and twenty essays on philosophy, ecology, literature, food, and music. He blogs regularly at http://www.ecologywithoutnature.blogspot.com.

Daniel Spencer is Professor of Environmental Studies at the University of Montana. His research interests are on community participation in ecological restoration, environmental and social justice issues connected to economic globalization, and the intersection of religion, ecology, and environmental ethics. His publications include: *Earth Ethics: A Case Method Approach* (with James B. Martin-Schramm and Laura Stivers) (Orbis

Press, 2015), and *Gay and Gaia: Ethics, Ecology and the Erotic* (Pilgrim Press, 1996).

Carol Wayne White is Professor of Philosophy of Religion at Bucknell University, and the author of *Poststructuralism, Feminism, and Religion: Triangulating Positions* (Humanity Books, 2002); *The Legacy of Anne Conway (1631–1670): Reverberations from a Mystical Naturalism* (SUNY Press, 2009); and *Black Lives and Sacred Humanity: Toward an African American Religious Naturalism* (Fordham, 2016). She has published articles on process philosophy, religious naturalism, and critical theory. White has also received national awards and fellowships, including an Oxford University Fellowship in Religion and Science, a Science and Religion Course Award Program Development Grant (The John Templeton Foundation), and a NEH Fellowship. She is currently writing a new book that explores the tenets of deep ecology and insights of religious naturalism expressed in contemporary American nature poets and writers.

·

www.ingramcontent.com/pod-product-compliance
Lightning Source LLC
Chambersburg PA
CBHW050654270326
41927CB00012B/3022